SCALE YOUR SMALL BUSINESS

THE DEFINITIVE GUIDE TO A SUSTAINABLE BUSINESS AND FULFILLING LIFE

BY LINDA CHUNG

ISBN-13: 978-1-7382081-0-4

ABOUT THE AUTHOR

Linda Chung, is a 25-year veteran of international corporations and now a professional business coach accredited by the International Coaching Federation. During this period, she has witnessed and interacted with many business leaders who suffer from poor work-life balance, low productivity, and lousy life fulfillment. It became clear to her that seeing financial success as an end in itself rather than a means to happiness did not make for thriving careers nor companies.

More importantly, she discovered ways we can all pursue holistic success. The result is the SCALE-UP system, which has enabled her clients to grow their businesses without sacrificing what's important to them. Linda is driven by her desire to help entrepreneurs build their businesses, legacy and ultimately prosperity.

Her personal goal is to help clients become their best selves. The practical importance of this cannot be overstated: most of the time, businesses are successful because of proper guidance and vision. Personal development makes it possible to provide these.

Her hobbies include gardening (sustainable of course), healthy (and spicy) cooking, studying, travelling, and meeting people from all walks of life and corners of the world. As she and her life partner, Håkan, are financially independent, they are also regular contributors to various effective charities.

Claim your surprise gift

Thank you for purchasing this book. It means a lot to me. To show my appreciation, I've prepared a special gift for you. Access it by visiting

www.sustainablelifedesign.com/thankyou

TABLE OF CONTENTS

INTRODUCTION

What Truly Drives Entrepreneurs?

Fulfillment. It is the unspoken motivation behind everything we do. The desire for fulfillment is what helps you keep the big picture in mind on days when twenty things are happening at once. It's what keeps you going when eventual success seems like a pipe dream. In fact, it's probably what caused you to venture into the world of business in the first place.

As business owners, our desires for productivity, growth, and even prosperity are only really means to an end – fulfillment. We want a satisfying life and a flourishing business that allows our team, clients, and ourselves to lead fulfilled lives. Making money is a key component of this goal; however, we shouldn't fall into the trap of seeing financial success as the main or only reason for going to work every day.

In fact, my life purpose is to help people to live more fulfilling lives. When I started my coaching business, I deliberately chose small businesses as my focus, exactly because there is an innate connection between business success and personal fulfillment. If, like my clients, you own a small business, you want to grow your company, boost productivity and profitability, and attain financial security. Really, though, this is only so you can pursue your dream lifestyle and enjoy ample time to do the things you love.

By helping my clients to build productive businesses, I endeavour to contribute to their fulfillment directly and, indirectly, that of their communities. Smaller enterprises have a lot more control over why they do what they do and how they go about their daily business. This means that, as entrepreneurs, we can find our own fulfillment while supporting that of our teams and improving our clients' lives. This is why I own a small business. I'm guessing the same applies to you, too, since you've picked up this book.

What exactly does leading a fulfilling life mean for you, though? As a business coach, a surprisingly large part of my job involves helping my clients define this. It is only once we've pinned down that rationale that we can start creating a plan to help you achieve fulfillment in your life by pursuing success in business. To state this another way: business success on its own isn't an end goal, but rather a stepping stone towards what's truly important – which is something each person has to decide for themselves.

It is my hope that this book will walk you through the process of paving a path toward your personal vision of fulfillment by identifying the right priorities and creating a productivity plan centred around those key objectives. All three of these elements – vision, priorities, and productivity – need to work together in a symbiotic relationship.

As you will see in the following chapters, choosing the right priorities allows your productivity to take you toward true fulfillment instead of further away from it. It is far easier to achieve productivity when you're working on tasks that you know will bring you prosperity. It becomes easier still when you start to reap the fruits of fulfillment. Finally, as you succeed in building a productive system and routine based on your priorities, you will inevitably start moving closer to your ultimate vision.

Reconciling Vision and Actions

So, how exactly do we get from here to there? Over the years, I've developed a system I call SCALE-UP. This has proven to be extraordinarily effective at giving my clients a blueprint for growing their small businesses while putting both their personal fulfillment and financial prosperity at the centre of their plans. This is an often-overlooked aspect of business planning: if you don't align your financial and personal objectives, there's a good chance that you'll end up disappointed in one aspect even if you succeed in the other.

This book will guide you through this SCALE-UP method. As you will see, the SCALE-UP system starts by identifying what a fulfilling life and prosperous company may look like to you. It then smoothly leads into identifying what changes you need to make to actualize those visions.

Personally, I'm careful to never make any impossible promises. While I am intimately familiar with what small businesses in general experience, I have no idea what's going on with your company, your goals, or the resources at your disposal. I know that I can't tell you exactly what kinds of success you may achieve. Just that you can. We all can.

I am, however, confident that you will gain knowledge that will help you identify some small or even major changes you can make, today and in the coming months, to bolster your sense of personal and professional fulfillment. I've seen it happen and have also learned to spot the pitfalls that can get in the way of success. This book is the product of experience – both mine and that of my clients – not wishful thinking or ivory-tower theories.

We will concentrate chiefly on creating sustainable growth. I can guarantee that focusing your routine and your business around your goals will lead you onto the path toward a more fulfilling life. You will be surprised at how powerful "focus" can be. A focused leader with a focused business will almost inevitably create extraordinary outcomes.

Rather than specifying every little step you need to take to build your business – after all, every organization is different – my aim for this book is to empower you to create and carry out a SCALE-UP plan tailored to your enterprise. At the end of each chapter, there will be action steps to guide you through implementing what you have just learned. I recommend allocating 30-60 minutes to plan these "actions" once you've finished each chapter. You can then use this blueprint to complete the necessary tasks throughout the week.

Knowledge without activity has no merits. In fact, it's better to read just one chapter and take one significant step based on what you learned in it rather than reading the entire book without doing anything new at all. To help you put this principle into practice, you will find a handy resources page to support you as well as several helpful exercises:

https://sustainablelifedesign.com/ScaleYourSmallBusiness

"Freedom lies in being bold." – Robert Frost

Are you willing to be bold enough to define your fulfillment vision and live your dream lifestyle?

Let's jump right in.

The SCALE-UP Framework at a Glance

"The summit is what drives us, but the climb itself is what matters." – Conrad Anker, American rock climber, mountaineer, and author.

It can help to think of your business's SCALE-UP framework a bit like a detailed plan for a challenging hike. I just mentioned that knowledge without action doesn't get you very far; it's equally true that simply doing something without a goal or a route toward it can get you into all sorts of mischief.

My partner Håkan and I are avid hikers. Fortunately, we live in BC, Canada, which is home to some of the world's most spectacular hiking trails. Even though we go on a lot of hikes, we always plan our adventures in advance, especially if we take on a difficult route.

Feeling in harmony with nature and experiencing all of its majestic beauty is what drives us to hike not only in our vicinity but also all around the world. We decide together which summit we are tackling and which trail to take, how much we plan to challenge ourselves, how long we'll stay out, and so on. We want the route to be within our capabilities and, by now, we have a pretty good idea of how long it takes to get to a chosen destination.

We can then use this knowledge to determine how much food and water we need to bring and decide what other gear will be necessary. Regardless of which hike we choose, we always take a compass/mobile phone, along with detailed route information and maps. And, of course, if we're hiking in BC, we'll bring our bear spray. Incidentally, we've never actually had to confront a bear in all of our hikes; however, Håkan believes this is precisely because we're carrying the spray.

Similarly, when we're "bushwalking" in Australia, Håkan carries a rather large stick which he alternately calls his "snake stick" or "poisonous spiderweb removal stick". Yes, he can be a little preoccupied with keeping us safe, which is why he loves "tramping" in New Zealand where the worst thing that can happen is being mobbed by a flock of sheep. Haha.

I'm a bit of a risk-taker, and he is obviously someone who believes in applying a little prudence. Knowing our individual strengths makes us a good team in hiking as well as in life. Needless to say, the better prepared we are, the more likely our hiking expeditions will be successful.

Hopefully, the above story provided you with a little bit of entertainment. The point, however, is to set out some parameters to anchor the rest of the discussion. Now, let's use our hiking example to illustrate how the SCALE-UP framework can be applied to your business:

- **Defining the Purpose:** Enjoying a little stress-free time in nature and experiencing its wonders are our main reasons for hiking. The PURPOSE answers the question: "Why?". Why are we doing this, even though we may get tired and develop blisters? In life and business, too, you need to define your own "why". Do you hope to impact the world, make a lot of money, help others, or be recognized as an expert in your field? Everything starts with your purpose.

- **Deciding on the Summit:** We don't just say: "Let's go hiking!" We first need to decide which DESTINATION to aim at and how we plan to achieve the climb. In order to achieve anything worthwhile, all of us need to be certain of what exactly we are trying to achieve. So, "I want to live my dream lifestyle" or "I want to grow my business" is not specific enough. We need to get absolute clarity about what that dream lifestyle looks like and what the growth of your business will entail.

- **Packing the Compass:** During our hike, there will be many deciding moments during which we ask ourselves: "Which way now?" Sometimes, we get completely lost. ("There are trees in every direction," as Håkan once famously said, which was accurate if not particularly helpful at the time.) This is why a compass, analogous to your CORE VALUES, is so important. We turn to our GPS to guide us along the most efficient route. In your business, your core values help you to decide if you are moving in the right direction or not, whether you're making a hiring decision or choosing an expansion strategy.

- **Preparing the Best Route Map:** If you want to reach your destination, it's best to ensure that you start in the right place, follow the map, and that you cross off your milestones as you reach them. The SCALE-UP framework will help you create business and personal goals along the way to your vision. It's incredibly helpful to define a PROCESS OF SUCCESS with timelines you can use to track how you move forward in the direction of success and fulfillment.

- **Assessing Your and Your Team's Capabilities:** List your assets and CORE STRENGTHS. Who can best organize your supplies and equipment? Read maps? Share the load according to each person's strengths and passion. Maybe one person is always the map reader while the other one surveys the terrain and keeps a watchful eye out for "snikes" (if you're Down Under) What does your organization do better than anyone else? How will you distribute responsibilities between departments or team members?

- **Selecting Your Team:** Depending on the scope of the expedition, you may need additional team members or to upgrade your current skills. In an unfamiliar environment, the right guide often makes the difference between a pleasant stroll and a backbreaking trek that ends with somebody in the hospital. Assembling an ELITE TEAM can make success possible even when the odds are against you.

- **Choosing the Right Gear:** Ensuring the success of your plan also relies on developing a PRODUCTIVITY SYSTEM. Just like you want sturdy hiking boots instead of flip-flops when making a challenging ascent, or avoid going on a hike without food and water, you have to set yourself and your team up for success by creating routines and systems that get things done efficiently.

- **Deciding on a Leader for the journey:** Even a one-person team requires LEADERSHIP; in this case, I call it self-leadership. We lead our clients and vendors even if no employees are involved. If you want to keep moving in the right direction rather than being passively pushed around by outside forces, this guiding role has to be acknowledged and accepted.

- **Getting Everyone on the Same Page:** Are your team members UNITED behind a strong vision and each aligned with the process you plan to follow during the journey? As a business owner, you will want everyone on board. If the hike was decided upon collectively, everyone on the team should be excited by its vision, goals, and processes. Involving the entire team in the planning process gives you the best chance of meaningful buy-in and, through that, success. Remember: this isn't just about you being able to take a selfie at the mountain's summit to post on social media, right? This is meant to be an epic group picture with everyone making it to the top, a little sweaty perhaps, but all smiling. That's the ultimate "unity" shot you're aiming for.

How to Use This Book

The above, in a nutshell, describes the SCALE-UP system. This book is organized into three sections to introduce you to the intricacies of implementing this framework.

Part I of the book establishes your self-leadership framework. It answers the question: "What makes you a productive person and ensures fulfillment?" Its goal is to provide you with a system based on your life purpose, vision, core values, and personal productivity routine.

Part II will help you build a successful business foundation. Here, we answer the question: "What makes a business thriving and profitable?" This section leads you through the process of defining your Core Strengths (business core purpose, core values, and core focus or specialization), your Ambitious Vision, Leadership, and Elite Team.

Finally, Part III gives actionable guidelines for walking the road to success. How do you ensure the actualization of your vision? What do you do when things seem to be drifting off the rails? This section offers proven advice on achieving organizational unity and developing strong processes.

Are you ready to get started?

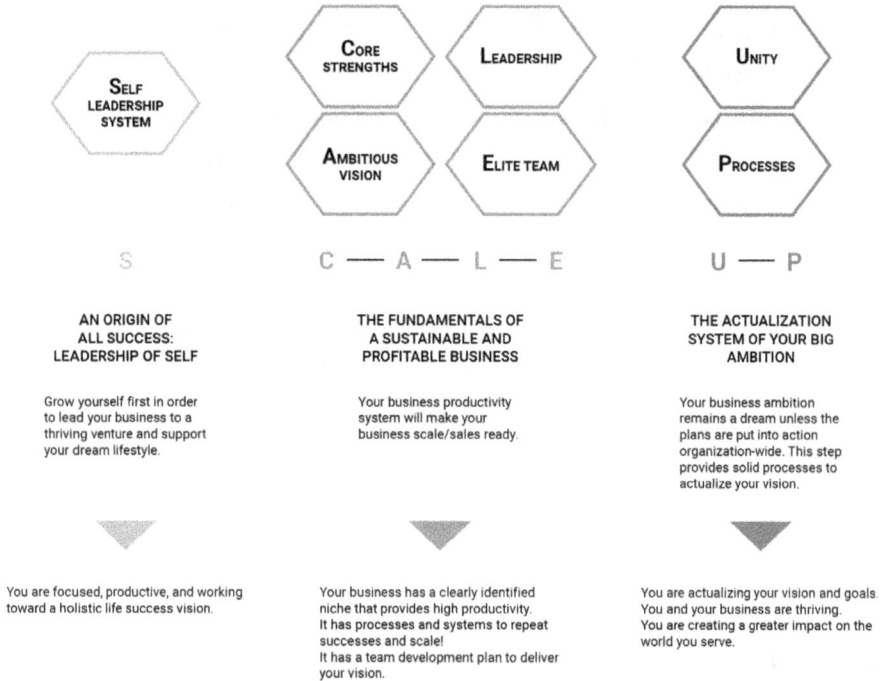

SELF LEADERSHIP SYSTEM	CORE STRENGTHS / AMBITIOUS VISION / LEADERSHIP / ELITE TEAM	UNITY / PROCESSES
S	C — A — L — E	U — P
AN ORIGIN OF ALL SUCCESS: LEADERSHIP OF SELF	**THE FUNDAMENTALS OF A SUSTAINABLE AND PROFITABLE BUSINESS**	**THE ACTUALIZATION SYSTEM OF YOUR BIG AMBITION**
Grow yourself first in order to lead your business to a thriving venture and support your dream lifestyle.	Your business productivity system will make your business scale/sales ready.	Your business ambition remains a dream unless the plans are put into action organization-wide. This step provides solid processes to actualize your vision.
You are focused, productive, and working toward a holistic life success vision.	Your business has a clearly identified niche that provides high productivity. It has processes and systems to repeat successes and scale! It has a team development plan to deliver your vision.	You are actualizing your vision and goals. You and your business are thriving. You are creating a greater impact on the world you serve.

\<The SCALE UP Framework\>

Your Action:

Prioritize Your SCALE-UP – Start planning your scale-up as a leader and entrepreneur

You're doing yourself no favours by pursuing narrow or ill-thought-out goals. Instead, you can follow the step-by-step system in this book to define your vision and keep all the aspects of your ideal life in harmony.

1. Commit 30 minutes to an hour of quiet time each day to planning actions after you've completed each chapter. Are you most productive first thing in the morning or late in the evening? Maybe the time of day when you're best able to focus and map things out is right after breakfast or a workout. Whatever may be the case, use this "golden time" to identify proactive ways of scaling up your personal and professional life.

PART I

LEAD YOURSELF FIRST
FOCUS ON YOURSELF BEFORE YOUR BUSINESS

"Knowing yourself is the beginning of all wisdom."

– Aristotle

During one course I took on my way to becoming an ICF-certified business coach, the instructor showed us two images to demonstrate a pearl of wisdom that's remained with me ever since. The first image was a small stick figure in front of an enormous boulder – we've all had days when we felt like our challenges were insurmountable.

The second image was of the same person, now much bigger, in fact towering over the boulder. *Something* has changed; she can now simply step over the obstacle if she chooses. The lesson here is that coaching is not so much about aiding people in solving their specific challenges but rather helping them grow to the point where they can overcome their obstacles on their own.

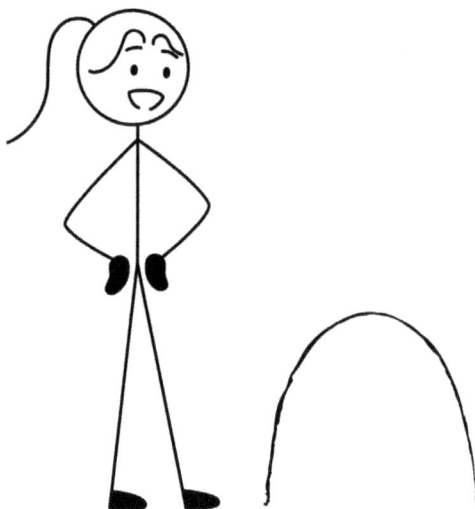

<Grow the Person>

Part One of the SCALE-UP system is therefore about what I like to call self-leadership, or growing yourself so that you can surmount whatever entrepreneurial challenges you may be faced with. This kind of growth starts with knowing and directing yourself, specifically in relation to your:

PURPOSE: What is the driving ambition in your life? This should be the key motivation behind your daily efforts and the life legacy you'll one day leave behind.

CORE VALUES: What are they? These guiding principles determine how you live your life in matters large and small.

VISION: What are the most important elements of your holistic concept of a successful life? This is the dream lifestyle that fulfills you.

PRODUCTIVITY SYSTEM: How will you actualize your fulfillment vision? This is your routine and framework for making a satisfying life a reality.

Starting the journey of building a successful venture without having the above elements in place is like sharing a boat with a rower who doesn't know where she is heading, with no navigation tools or boating skills. We won't even know what the journey is about, much less where we're going to end up. In this metaphor, the boat is your small business – the means to your chosen end. It's a tool to get you to your destination – an important tool that will absorb a lot of your energy and intention, but in principle no more important than a hammer. Your business is a path to your fulfilling life, not a purpose in itself.

Now, a much better scenario is one in which your little vessel is guided by your North Star (your purpose), you know where you are heading (your fulfillment vision), and have a compass (core values) to point you in the right direction at crucial decision-making moments. To this, you need to add the skills necessary to row the boat (a productivity system). Your odds of arriving at your destination will be far greater than otherwise. You will also get there faster and more efficiently. Yet, how many of us have taken the boat out onto the water without even thinking about these crucial elements?

You may ask, "What does my personal life have to do with growing my business? This is meant to be a business book after all, not life coaching!"

The simple fact is that there are psychological processes that affect all of us in roughly the same ways. You can, of course, ignore these, just like you can base all your plans on the assumption that water will flow uphill. Any success you achieve by doing so, however, will only be accidental.

On the other hand, using your character, your genuine goals, and the realities of your personal life as a starting point for all your plans ensures that your business is serving your sense of fulfillment, not the other way around. This allows you to figure out how to shape your organization so that it supports what is truly important to you, both now and later. With this foundation in place, you as a business owner will be driven by passion and fulfillment – the same passion and fulfillment that you will build your company culture around, as outlined in future chapters.

Looking inward before you leap outward helps you to be a more effective leader. When you, as the one at the helm of your business, are clear on your chosen purpose, core values, and vision, you can create an organization aligned and compatible with them. This harmony creates a powerful synergy where your personal wins benefit the business, and business success benefits you in your personal life.

Just like the boat is an important tool needed to carry you to your destination, your organization is a tool to help you build a life you can be proud of. However, what we want to achieve needs to be determined before we even begin worrying about the shape of the boat. The alternative – starting a company without any idea of our life purpose – generally means ending up in a place you never wanted to be after a journey that was sheer drudgery.

If you don't determine your own destination, society (and perhaps well-intended friends) will impose theirs on you, perhaps without you even realizing until it's too late. Conversely, when we choose our destinations based on what fulfills each of us and are firmly guided by our own reasons, the right people will inevitably turn up along the way to support our journey.

The first step to achieving this alignment is to understand who you are at your very core.

CHAPTER 1

LIFE PURPOSE – YOUR NORTH STAR, WHY, AND PURPOSE

"You cannot get through a single day without having an impact on the world around you. What you do makes a difference, and you have to decide what kind of difference you want to make."

– Jane Goodall, Anthropologist, Primatologist,
Author, Amazing Human

Entrepreneurs are driven to start businesses for a wide variety of reasons. When you get right down to it, though, these pretty much boil down to what we can offer the world through our productive efforts and the advantages owning a business offers us in turn.

One of my clients (we'll call her Lucy) started an education consultancy firm because she saw a gap in the market that coincided with a chance to serve a good cause. Specifically, she decided to guide youths to success by helping them pursue life-enhancing education opportunities overseas. Her company operates as a matchmaker between Canadian schools and adventurous international students, helping them select the most appropriate study programs.

As we discussed the concept of individual purpose, however, Lucy realized that her daily actions were not aligned with the reason she started her business in the first place. You see, her company held individual contracts with different schools. Naturally, each one worked on a different compensation model. Some institutions paid higher commissions for successful student referrals than others.

Without even realizing it, Lucy and her team had become entangled in a profit-first culture and were beginning to see student placements as a cash cow. She had set out with noble aims, but now they were recommending schools based on earnings instead of the impact they could have on young lives.

Lately, Lucy had started to feel unfulfilled and unmotivated. It felt like day-in and day-out she was dealing with student complaints, high rates of employee turnover, and a lack of productivity. She came to me for coaching because her work was a major stressor. Worse, that stress was beginning to seep into other areas of her life. She had started a rewarding, fulfilling business; somewhere along the way, it had morphed into something other than what she'd intended.

There are at least two reasons why Lucy strayed so far from her original intention. With the main purpose unidentified, the easiest thing to grab onto – and an eminently worthy goal by society's standards – is money. In the absence of our own specifically designated purposes, we are likely to take on a motivation borrowed from others – profit. For Lucy, this accidental shift in focus created an environment exactly opposite to her initial dream of helping youth pursue life-enhancing education opportunities. Imagine a boat that's taking an easy route by following other boats rather than going to its planned destination.

The second reason is that she never clearly determined her life purpose. When Lucy started her business, she had some ideas about how she wanted to impact her clients' lives, but she never quite got around to defining these in specific terms. I see this often in entrepreneurs with children who started their businesses in order to provide the best for their families. The tricky thing is that they often don't have a clear idea of what that "best" looks like, so they simply accept the definition society gives them – making lots of money. This is how many business-owning parents end up sacrificing time with their families in pursuit of a materialistic dream they never chose for themselves.

Many times, working with these clients to clarify what they mean by providing the best for their family, it quickly becomes clear that they want to be there for their kids as loving parents. They want to share in their achievements and spend meaningful time with their children. Neither they nor their kids see material gifts as a good substitute for their love; these are merely stand-ins for when you can't provide the real thing.

Having a clear life purpose helps you to navigate these choices when they arise. Combined with core values, vision, and productivity, your purpose provides you with a decision-making matrix that helps you balance your priorities. This allows you to grow professionally and personally with intent rather than chasing growth for the sake of growth.

Before Lucy decided on her business purpose, she needed to be clear about her life purpose. Once this was established, she could redefine her business goals to support the greater ambition of personal fulfillment. This alignment helps her stay on track and improves the odds of getting to the destination she chose for herself. In your own life, too, building this kind of structure will make it much, much easier to make daily progress toward your purpose while also enjoying a fulfilling journey.

What Is a Life Purpose?

It may seem inconceivable that something as intangible as a life purpose can have such a huge impact on our day-to-day activities. In reality, a life purpose is like the North Star: an ever-present beacon providing us with constant guidance throughout our lives.

Imagine you are up for a promotion at work. On the surface, this may seem like a simple decision. Why wouldn't anyone want to accept a fancier title and the salary increase that comes with it? However, different people may well see this choice in different lights based on their life purposes, along with their visions and values.

If your life purpose is to provide the best quality care for your loved ones, and you define that as being fully present in their lives, a promotion that comes with longer hours and frequent work trips may not be the best option.

If your life purpose is to make a bigger impact on your community and colleagues, and the promotion allows you to do just that, then the answer may be a clear yes.

If your life purpose involves learning skills that the new position will expose you to, accepting the promotion seems like a good idea. If you'll receive greater satisfaction from a side business you run in your free time, your priorities may dictate that you say no and keep your schedule free.

Knowing your life purpose makes these kinds of choices easy because it gives you a way to measure the weight of each pro and con of the options in front of you. It highlights points of friction between your purpose and life's demands. Instead of being passively led by what society tells you you should value or what the people around you would choose, you can make decisions that help you to live a fulfilling life according to your own definition.

> Life's purpose is our individual North Star. It is what gives life meaning, and it helps us stay grounded when the going gets rough. Our life purpose informs our decisions, supports our growth, and gives strength to those around us.

Having a life purpose also makes it easier to work towards the goals you believe in. Doing what is necessary becomes less painful because you can see that your efforts matter in the long run. This is true whether you are making a contribution to a global cause or whether you are making time to go to your child's basketball game. Neither of these things is inherently more important than the other – you have to choose your purpose and priorities yourself. In many cases, making that kind of decision still requires courage, but knowing your purpose makes identifying the right option a lot simpler.

Let's jump back to my client Lucy. The very first thing we did in coaching was to clarify and define her life purpose so it could inform her decision-making. What we came up with was "to empower young people to build successful lives". Her business's purpose is to support and help Latin American youths access quality education and secure solid careers through her overseas education consulting work. (Your business purpose may look entirely different; a process for defining this is further explored in a later chapter in Part II.)

As we can see in Lucy's example, a life purpose is usually not brand new to us. Defining it doesn't require any special insight or profound realization. It's normally a dormant force within us, just waiting to be clarified and brought to life. The trick here is that, once your purpose is given a name, it takes on its full potency. While it's still unidentified and nameless, your purpose isn't very useful. As in Lucy's case, leaving your purpose undefined makes it easy to drift off track.

Now that it's been set in place, Lucy's purpose guides her in all her major decisions: her life and business vision, her relationships, and all other aspects of her life. She now has her North Star, her ever-present guide, and lives according to a purpose she chose and defined on her own terms.

She's now decisive when selecting which of her partner schools to send her students to. Do they have a track record of delivering quality education and ensuring career success for their students? Do they consistently satisfy the clients she refers to them? Can they boast the right kind of leadership and the support structures international students need? Note that these objectives, while perfectly aligned with Lucy's business purpose, aren't in any way incompatible with making money. Using your life purpose to guide your decisions can, in fact, improve your productivity and profitability way more than any focus on short-term gains.

Today, both Lucy and her employees are clear about the business's culture and purpose. This kind of cohesiveness also represents an opportunity to attract current and future employees who share these values. Profit-centred individuals tend to screen themselves out, while employees who find fulfillment in promoting student success are enthusiastic about the company.

Students flock to Lucy's consulting business because of her reputation. She automatically attracts the clients she needs to further grow her business.

Looked at in the short term, during particular periods, her company may not appear to be the most profitable. Taking a broader view, however, it follows a sustainable growth model that ensures productivity with the right purpose, the right team, and the right clientele (among other things that just seem to "fall into place"). It also provides a fulfilling journey as she and her team constantly hear success stories from her students and school partners instead of complaints. Their work is meaningful. Almost everything they do is fulfilling now and in the long term.

Discovering Your Life Purpose

Given how large an impact your life purpose can have on every aspect of what you do each day, defining it can seem like a hopelessly difficult task. Admittedly, it is a big question to answer, especially if you've never really thought in those terms.

Just as a buried treasure lies hidden beneath the surface, our true passions, potential, and purpose may be concealed beneath layers of daily routines and societal expectations. Delving into the depths of self-discovery and personal growth is akin to excavating that treasure, revealing the valuable insights and aspirations that can guide us toward a more meaningful and fulfilling existence. So, how can we accomplish this?

There's a particular exercise I like to use to help my clients find their life purpose. Imagine that you are celebrating a life well lived to a ripe old age, and it is time to commemorate it with the people who matter the most to you. You are eating, drinking, and dancing with a whole crowd: some may even be people whom you've never met but whose lives you impacted positively in some way. Others have known you for years and may have travelled long distances to celebrate with you. Visualize what this gathering would look like.

Start by picturing the location of the party. You can think of a specific location if you have one in mind or think of a general setting like a fancy hotel ballroom, the seaside, or maybe a country cottage. As the guest of honour, the location will be meaningful to you. Concentrate on the experience of being in those surroundings. What do you see? What do you smell? What do you hear? How do you feel about the event?

Throughout the event, people are mingling and swapping stories about you. Some are funny, some will probably be embarrassing but, mostly, people are sharing tales of how you touched their lives. What kinds of things would you like them to say about you?

It can help to think about the people who matter to you in four groups: family, friends, people you work with, and people you affect indirectly. Don't forget to include people you have only interacted with online in those groups.

- What would you like them to say about the kind of person you are?

- What would you like them to say about the work you did?

- What would you like them to say about your impact on their lives?

- What would you like them to say about your impact on the world?

Write down everything that comes to mind, even if it seems irrelevant. This exercise brings what is significant to you into sharp focus. You can see which people are important to you and what you want to achieve in life – your well-lived, ideal life.

Once you have a long list of things people would say about you, it's time to see what wisdom we can gain from our invited guests. Decide which entries on the list resonate with you. Which ones make you feel proud to think about? Which ones make you smile? Which ones make you feel fulfilled?

Is there a common theme in your list? As in Lucy's case, perhaps there is one overriding impulse that has been lying, dormant and unacknowledged, in the background until now. She has always wanted to support the youth. You'll know you're close to finding your life purpose when you start to think about certain past events as part of a much larger pattern. A compliment that someone gave you years ago may come to mind. You'll suddenly realize why you were strongly drawn to a friend or why a particular conversation you once had stuck so vividly in your mind.

Some examples of life purpose that I see among my clients are:

- Serving their community in meaningful ways
- Creating positive change in the world
- Pursuing a life of self-discovery
- Investing energy into relationships with family, friends, and colleagues
- Making a difference in the life of someone else
- Help people feel heard and seen as they truly are

Many of my clients share my life purpose of helping, guiding, and supporting people through their capabilities, passions, and beliefs. They may do this to serve their God, for the joy of creating something, or due to their passion for travelling and the expanded horizons that come from experiencing new places and cultures. I am passionate about living a fulfilling life, and my coaching business enables me to help people in a way that is meaningful to me and plays to my strengths. This job allows me to apply my capability for productivity, business and people development, and my deeply held belief that we all have the freedom to choose what our lives will look like. I help others build businesses that allow them to live their dream lives.

What I have found from my own experience and through helping entrepreneurs and leaders create fulfilling lives is this: when we know our life purpose, it gives us clarity on the kind of life we want to create for ourselves. It helps us make meaningful connections with others and forges a greater sense of belonging. These are benefits you will see in your everyday life as well as in your business.

Claim Your Life Purpose

Take a moment to define your life purpose before you move on to the next chapter. What is important to you and what kind of legacy do you want to leave behind? Considering your passions, beliefs, and capabilities, what is the driving ambition that gives you a meaningful directional guide in your life?

As already mentioned, my own life purpose can be stated as "to help people live their most fulfilling lives". This provides direction to my day-to-day work, among other things. Through my coaching, I help business owners and leaders lead more purposeful lives, including through their thriving organizations. I also use a part of my proceeds to practice philanthropy, volunteer, and mentor people in various ways. All of these activities can be interpreted as working towards my life purpose.

You will define your life purpose in different ways throughout your life; expect it to evolve and don't be afraid of refining it as time goes by. So, don't spend too much time wordsmithing or nitpicking. The only thing that matters is that your life purpose speaks to you and motivates you in the here and now.

Your Action:

Define and Name Your Life Purpose: Decide what is genuinely important to you and what you want to achieve.

All of us have a life purpose. This often involves helping others. Nevertheless, until you can articulate it, you're bound to ignore it sometimes when a decision is called for. Thinking about what your loved ones may say once you've achieved it can give you greater clarity.

1. Spend some time today on discovering your life purpose. Using the "well-lived life celebration" visualization exercise, brainstorm what matters most to you. What types of comments will make you happy or proud to hear coming from the people in your life? Almost certainly, the theme that connects these things closely resembles your life purpose. We will work on your business purpose in a future chapter, so just focus on your life purpose for the moment.

CHAPTER 2

CORE VALUES – YOUR INTERNAL COMPASS, GUIDING PRINCIPLES, AND HOW TO LIVE TRUE TO YOURSELF

"Every life is a dilemma that must be solved by the person living it."

— Jo Coudert, American Author

The average person makes tens of thousands of decisions each day. Many of those decisions put very little at stake, like whether you have one more cup of coffee before you leave the house. We make these almost without thinking – whether you put on black or brown shoes in the morning affects virtually nothing. Other choices impact your business or your personal life in a far more significant way. These, naturally, require you to focus more closely.

As every leader and entrepreneur knows, though, constantly making decisions is exhausting. Sometimes, you need courage to choose the right path and have to confront the temptation to take the easy or familiar way out. Anything that makes this process simpler and less demanding is definitely worth looking at.

You've already made a start on building a more rational, efficient decision-making framework by defining your life purpose. Like the North Star, this gives you a clear picture of the general direction you're heading. This only provides part of the solution, however: you also need to know if any given decision will take you closer to or further away from your life purpose. This calls for another kind of navigational tool; one that can be applied to all areas of your life.

Your Core Values: Your Internal Compass

Your core values act like a compass, always telling you which of several possible choices is the most efficient path to the fulfilling life you aspire to. These principles or character traits are rooted in and support self-awareness around your strengths, weaknesses, and motivations. This, in turn, leads to greater self-confidence, resilience, and clarity in decision-making.

Before Laura started her education consulting business, she worked as a counsellor in a school. She loved her job and was very loyal to her employer, but there was a problem: she was constantly being put in situations where she had to sacrifice time with her family to complete her work.

Laura was not receiving the support she needed to get everything done during regular working hours. Being saddled with too many tasks for which she carried sole responsibility led to long hours. When she finally did get home, she didn't have much energy left. She felt like she couldn't give her son and husband the time and attention they deserved. Though this wasn't her fault, Laura felt almost constant guilt over not being there for her family as much as she wanted.

She had asked her boss multiple times to give her the resources she needed to achieve a better balance between her work and her personal life. Every time, she received a lukewarm response and, unsurprisingly, no changes were made. She was serving her life purpose of helping young people achieve their potential, but this environment was not compatible with her core values. In her case, following her personal North Star was not enough: she needed to calibrate her internal compass, too.

Once we identified her core values, it was as if everything fell into place. "Family" ranked extremely high on her list of fundamental motivations. She also valued respect and fairness. Once she could see this information in black and white, it became clear why she was feeling frustrated and unfulfilled. She was devoted to her job but not receiving anything in return, all the while sacrificing something important to her for no real reward. She had told me that she had a long-held ambition to start her own business, and after uncovering her core values, it was clear which direction she should take.

She wasn't ready to quit her job right away, however. Laura wanted to get to a place where she could start her own business without jeopardizing her financial stability. It wasn't too early to take the first steps, though. We were able to sketch out a plan that identified when she would feel stable enough to leave. Once this was made clear, we could figure out what she needed to do to reach that point as quickly as possible.

Understanding her core values helped Laura recognize that her work was not bringing her fulfillment. With no significant changes on the horizon, it was time to leave. Of course, knowing what you should do and taking the necessary action aren't quite the same thing. Acknowledging the ideals that are most important to her also gave Laura some much-needed clarity about the decision and furnished her with the confidence she needed to move forward.

What Are Your Core Values?

When we are not aware of our core values, life is much harder than it needs to be. Dilemmas are a feature of daily life: should I go with A or B? Will trying to impress my boss bring me an advantage, or is developing my hobbies the key to happiness?

This kind of uncertainty can be stifling, and not just because of the mental overhead involved in making any complicated decision. We often end up choosing the path of least resistance, and this tends to be the status quo instead of what may be best for us. And, sometimes, we are simply paralyzed by options, either having too many or none that seem attractive. That is what happened to Laura and, in fact, what happens to many of us. Making a deliberate choice and taking appropriate, purposeful action often takes far too long, robbing us of happiness that's actually well within our grasp.

Core values are the bedrock of who we are and what we stand for. They provide a foundation for all our decisions and actions. Simply recognizing them helps us steer our lives in the right direction.

Looked at from this perspective, knowing our core values is essential to building a business that supports our vision of a fulfilling life. It is these principles that guide us in organizing our resources and routines around what we stand for and what is truly important to each of us. Here are some examples of core values. This is not a complete list, but it makes for a good starting point. As you read them, make a note of any that resonate with you.

Accountability	Empathy	Logic
Adaptability	Enthusiasm	Love
Altruism	Equality	Loyalty
Assertiveness	Fairness	Openness
Balance	Fidelity	Optimism
Boldness	Freedom	Patience
Calm	Fun	Passion
Candour	Generosity	Persistence
Charity	Gratitude	Playfulness
Common sense	Happiness	Purposefulness
Compassion	Harmony	Realism
Confidence	Health	Respect
Connection	Honesty	Responsibility
Consistency	Honour	Security
Conviction	Hope	Self-reliance
Cooperation	Humility	Selfless
Courage	Humour	Service
Creativity	Individuality	Tolerance
Decisiveness	Inspiration	Transparency
Dependability	Intelligence	Trustworthiness
Discipline	Integrity	Understanding
Drive	Justice	Unity
Efficiency	Kindness	

You may have noticed that some of these words are almost synonyms. Take generosity and charity, for example: their meanings overlap in most cases but diverge in some. Later in this chapter, we will discuss how to make sure you pick the right option among similar core values. For now, unless you feel like poring over a dictionary, just choose whichever one you feel is the best fit.

Mine Your Values

Many of us feel (or used to feel) like we're being pulled in a dozen different directions every time we have to make a choice. The inevitable result is that we end up getting in our own way whenever it's time to take positive action. If this sounds like a common problem in your life, it may simply be that you've never had a chance to examine which ideals matter most to you.

The good news is that everyone already possesses a set of core values. They are most certainly there, perhaps just hidden under the surface of your personality. At most, you just have yet to dig them out and give them names.

One interesting characteristic of core values is that they're what connect you to your peak moments. What makes certain events so elating? Pretty generally, this happens when your actions and experiences align with what you value most. Conversely, your core values often lie behind moments of deep hurt or upsetting life events. Why do two people experience the same event, but one person is greatly upset by it while the other person remains indifferent? It is often because of a difference in core values.

Let's say your workplace suddenly abandons flexitime and work-from-home arrangements and starts requiring all employees to clock in at 8:30 a.m. sharp. Someone whose core values include freedom and integrity will probably feel insulted. The person who sits at the desk next to them, who puts great stock in discipline and security, may instead see this as a change for the better. Being sensitive to the core values of others, by the way, is far from the worst quality a manager can have.

This chapter is all about assembling the internal compass that you will use for the rest of the journey that is your life. Understand that, as with your life purpose, defining the core values that make up this compass is really about self-discovery, not deciding what "ought" to be important to you. Accepting values imposed from the outside is unlikely to ever lead to happiness.

I'm now going to walk you through five exercises that will help you uncover your core values. These thought experiments have been drawn from various sources; my clients have found them very useful as tools to learn more about their fundamental motivations. Before continuing, grab a notebook and find somewhere quiet to sit down and think through these exercises.

Exercise 1: What Have Been the Peak Experiences of Your Life?

As I mentioned, moments of great joy provide a valuable window into our core values. We're talking about those times when you thought "This is the best day of my life," "It doesn't get any better," or "I was born for this."

Now, what about the event or moment made it so elating and memorable? It may be helpful to remember what sounds you were hearing, what you saw, and the scents that caught your attention. The focus, however, should be on the uplifting feelings you enjoyed during and after the event.

Let me give you an example of how this works. One of my own peak experiences was standing on stage in front of a few hundred people at my company's 20-year anniversary celebration. I was giving a speech to our staff and VIP clients in the audience. As I looked around, I could see a sea of smiling faces and sense their pride in our shared achievements.

When I think about why this is a peak moment in my life, the first thing that comes to mind is the incredible sense of accomplishment. Two decades prior, we had started out as a local Canadian company with exactly one product line. Now, we had become a global brand with multiple revenue streams and a solid history of industry recognition, respect, and accolades.

The second thing that stands out to me is how vividly I remember the people who shared in this achievement. This was a collective success involving both our team and key clients, and it felt great celebrating it with all of them.

Finish up the exercise by examining the values you associate with the experience. It doesn't need to be a business event: a precious moment spent with your family or a victory on the sports field can be equally valid. From the memory I just described, I can identify achievement, teamwork, and community as values present in that peak experience. Using the list above as a guide and pencilling in your own additions as necessary, try to connect your emotions with common standards and ideals.

You may find that more than one peak experience comes to mind when you do this exercise. If that's the case, repeat it for each of your fondest, proudest memories. Again, not all of them have to be related to your career; think back on the greatest wins in your personal life, too. The core values these help you discover may be more useful in business than you imagine. Also, not all peak experiences need to be on a grand scale, such as receiving an award or winning a championship. It could be something simpler, like finally learning how to swim, or organizing a meaningful event for your parents' golden wedding anniversary.

Exercise 2: What Makes You Angry?

On the opposite end of the emotional spectrum, intense feelings of anger, grief, or frustration can also be good indicators of the most important aspects of your character.

Think back to moments where you felt, in hindsight, that you had gotten irrationally annoyed or upset. Try to uncover the trigger behind these emotions, then examine how it relates to a particular core value that wasn't respected or honoured at the time. In the first exercise, we identified values that make you happy when they're allowed to flourish. Approaching the question from the opposite direction isn't as pleasant, but it's equally illuminating.

For example, if fairness is one of your core values and you were put in a situation that seemed unjust, you would feel unfulfilled, discontented, and quite possibly angry. So, if (for instance) you notice that you are constantly being ignored at work or treated as if your opinion doesn't matter, the injustice of the situation will torment you out of all proportion to the objective weight of the circumstances.

Those times when we feel anger boiling deep inside us over a seemingly trivial inconvenience are warnings that we're out of alignment with our core values in some way. In that sense, this kind of thing is not trivial at all. You just uncovered a core value that's being stepped on. Finding the common theme or thread in these memories will help us identify our values.

Exercise 3: Who Do You Admire?

Think about the people you look up to. They could be public figures or perhaps individuals in your own life. What specifically do you cherish about them?

A lot of my clients, for example, think highly of their parents and will mention either their father or mother during this exercise. They may admire their hardworking attitude, their compassion, their calmness under pressure, or their loving nature. Seeing or reading about actions or words that embody a value we hold dear resonates with us on a profound level. We want that characteristic to be present in our own words and deeds, so we can't help but look up to people who live that kind of life.

While doing this exercise, it's important not to be swayed by social pressure or hero worship. Many people who achieved greatness in some aspect of their lives had Achilles' heels in other ways, just like even the worst villains have a few redeeming qualities. There's nothing wrong with appreciating the positive aspects of someone's personality while also recognizing their flaws. In other words, once you begin to drill down, the emphasis of this exercise changes from "Who Do You Admire?" to "What values do you admire in the people you look up to?"

Exercise 4: What Are Important Elements for Fulfillment in Your Life?

Beyond your basic human needs, what must you have in your life to experience satisfaction and fulfillment? Here, we're talking about values like passion, creativity, or fun.

The goal of this exercise is to uncover any character traits that are important to your happiness but may not have been prominent in the key memories you examined. If your mind turns to commonplace essentials like "a good night's sleep" or "spending time with colleagues after hours", there's a good chance that these can be distilled into more abstract values. Try to search out common threads. If you're always happy at the end of a workday in which you met a demanding deadline or put a difficult customer at ease, integrity, accountability, or responsibility may be essential parts of your internal compass.

Håkan, my partner, is often the joke teller in various gatherings and brings levity to even life's tough situations. Humour and playfulness are important components of his life fulfillment. He has also been creating his own music ever since he was a child; creativity is a long-embodied value of his.

What about yours? What simple activities in your daily life consistently bring you joy and satisfaction, and what core values are they rooted in?

Exercise 5: What Quotes Do You Cherish?

What famous sayings and quotations hold a lot of meaning for you? It could be something said by a famous person or something that a person close to you once said that stuck in your mind. Which words of wisdom do you think about often and perhaps find yourself repeating to other people? Maybe it's even something you made up on your own.

These phrases are memorable precisely because they capture a value that you hold dear. For example, Håkan's favourite quote is from his holiness the Dalai Lama: "Be kind whenever possible. It's always possible." People often tell him that he is one of the kindest people they have ever met. Not surprisingly, kindness is his number one value. Mine is "Change is the only constant in life." I value adaptability and flexibility, and have learned to appreciate the transient nature of life.

Once you have your quote, think about the values that quote illustrates. You may well find that this thought experiment causes you to circle back to exercise 3 above, namely reflecting on who you admire. Franklin D. Roosevelt, for instance, famously said: "The only thing we have to fear is fear itself." This ties in perfectly with some of the core values he lived by, such as enthusiasm, boldness, and purposefulness.

Prioritizing and Ranking Your Core Values

Once you've worked through the five exercises above, you will probably have a long list of principles and character traits. Everybody values a lot of different things in themselves and the people around them; it would be hard to say you're actively opposed to any entry on our list. Still, for each and every one of us, some values are going to be more crucial than others. Your core values are those you consider most important of all; the needle in your internal compass.

Look back through your list of values and see which ones resonate with you on the most profound level. Which are true guiding principles in your life, not just characteristics you sometimes aspire to? Which are so funda-mental to your self-image, you would feel ashamed if you neglected them?

Let's try to narrow down all those you've written down to a shortlist of five. These are your core values. Selecting them can be difficult, but try to be as honest as possible with yourself. Remember: what we're actually doing is building a framework that will enhance and simplify all your decision-making going forward, whether in business, your relationships, and every other sphere you can think of. Striking some value off your core list doesn't mean you're rejecting it, just that displaying some other char-acteristic brings you greater fulfillment. Håkan, for instance, appreciates drive in himself and those he meets. If he's forced to choose between being driven or being kind, though, he'll choose kindness nine times out of ten.

The next step is to rank your core values in order of importance. This is absolutely necessary: life isn't always straightforward and you will face situ-ations in which your guiding principles aren't entirely compatible. Imagine that two of your core values are "family" and "achievement". Most of the time, these values don't come into conflict, as you can create a work-life balance that allows you to honour both kinds of obligations. On occasion, though, special circumstances at work or in your family may force you to prioritize one over the other.

For example, let's say you have a demanding client who is insisting on an expedited turnaround time. Instead of the week this task normally takes, they insist on getting it done in two days. Your "service" core value inclines you to say yes, but your "family" core value makes you hesitant to agree. What do you do when that happens?

The answer lies in which core value is higher in your hierarchy. Either way, you'll have to make a sacrifice. The important thing is to ensure this sacrifice is something you can afford according to your own value system.

Someone who prioritizes "service to others" over "family" might decide to say yes to a two-day turnaround time. They will then have a conversation with their family about why this work is important. They may even choose not to come home for a couple of days if that's what is needed to ensure delivering the work on time and to a high standard of quality.

By contrast, a person whose "family" core value trumps "service" might decide to say no to the expedited turnaround time and assert that one week is the best they can do. Even if this meant losing the client, they would be content due to the high importance they place on family.

These are two extreme examples of how a conflict between different core values might play out. Most situations that require you to balance one principle against another aren't as black-and-white. These decisions are rarely all-or-nothing affairs. To use an analogy, if I ranked my favourite foods in the same way I do my core values, chocolate cake will beat out asparagus – but this doesn't mean I always choose confectionery over vegetables.

Still, letting a few exaggerated scenarios play out in your imagination can help you identify how your core values rank. How, for instance, did you react to each of those examples? Did you find yourself thinking: "I'd never sacrifice family time to appease a demanding client," or did you lean towards: "I wouldn't say no to a client who needs help; after all, the money I'll earn is to support my family"?

Playing devil's advocate like this will help you see where each core value falls in your personal hierarchy. When I work with clients on ranking their core values, we generally start by brainstorming situations where their core values may collide and see which one they choose the majority of the time.

Knowing the hierarchy of your core values allows you to structure your life so that you can honour what's most important to you. Returning to the "family" vs. "service to others" example, someone who places a high emphasis on her "family" core value may arrange the way she works to allow prioritization of her home life. She could, for instance, write a minimum turnaround time into all her business contracts, safeguarding her time with her family. Should a client try to negotiate work on a shorter timeframe, she would already know how quickly she can finish the project without having to work excessive overtime or delivering low-quality work.

Someone else may well consider "service to others" as the more worthy. Note that preferring one hierarchy of core values to another doesn't make one person better than another. Within some very broad limits, every individual's principles are valid; it takes all kinds of people to make the world go round.

In this case, she may instead have a conversation about how she and her family can create a balance where she can prioritize their work without neglecting her obligations at home. This might involve building a support network of family, friends, and paid help to allow her to spend extra time on her business when necessary while knowing her family is being taken care of. Finding workarounds such as these also means that she can focus on quality time with her family when her work's demands allow.

It's incredibly important to rank your core values because, as the saying goes, knowledge is power. By understanding how you will prioritize your core values when put in situations where they are in opposition, you immediately reduce the amount of mental overhead and soul-searching needed to make a decision when this problem arises.

More importantly, this allows you to build systems into your life and business that strike a better balance between those core values. Once this is done, you won't often find yourself being forced to neglect one core value in favour of another.

Words Matter a Lot in Your Core Values

Before we move on, let's take another look at the core values you have identified. Several can be called by more than one name, or are confusingly similar to others. Considering how important your hierarchy of core values will be going forward, it pays to be as precise as possible.

Consider tolerance and openness, for instance. They overlap in a Venn diagram. There are some parts of openness and tolerance that are very similar. However, these two concepts are not identical – in fact, they're sometimes completely opposite. Being accessible to others doesn't necessarily mean accepting aspects of their behaviour that are irreconcilable with one of your core values, for instance.

Most of the time, this kind of thing isn't an issue. Your core values only need to be meaningful to you; it doesn't matter if your interpretation matches the dictionary definition of some word. What does matter is whether or not you are being guided by the right intention and can articulate it if necessary.

As an example, two of my clients, business partners Mark and Paula, indicated that transparency was a shared personal core value and was therefore going to be a core value of their business. Mark and Paula live and operate their business in Latin America. Culturally, trust cannot always be taken for granted, so transparency was important to them as a way to build solid relationships with their staff and customers. They knew that showing they were straightforward would increase customer acquisition and loyalty.

Mark and Paula needed to decide whether "trust" or "transparency" would better capture the essence of what they had in mind. Also, considering the meaning of each term, which could they deliver on most consistently? I asked them the following questions to guide them through this process:

- Which word would serve your business purpose better?

- Under what circumstances might you find it challenging to deliver on each value?

Through these questions, they realized that there were limits to how far they could commit to transparency. In practical terms, they wouldn't be able to hold themselves accountable to that value. They would not feel completely comfortable with total transparency around their staff's salary or incentive information, for instance, and frequently making common-sense exceptions to their own principle would only erode its significance. Trust, on the other hand, didn't present such challenges, so they found it to be a better fit.

Sometimes, defining your core values as accurately as possible is absolutely worth it. Just like ranking them relative to one another, it helps to imagine different possible scenarios while doing so.

Establish Guiding Principles for Your Core Values

Core values matter only when they have a genuine, palpable influence on our everyday lives. Only then are we fulfilled! Don't, in other words, treat this chapter as an academic exercise. That would be like trying to get into shape by paying for a gym membership and never actually working out.

One way to bring these values into our lives on a concrete, tangible level is to attach guiding principles to each one. No matter how careful-ly you define and rank your core values, terms like "decisiveness" and "self-reliance" remain a little abstract. We need something to tie theory and practice together.

If you think about the meaning that any of your core values holds for you, how can you make that come alive in your life? At this time, write one to three bullet points to define what the core value looks like in terms of what you do each day.

My own top five core values, for example, are freedom, integrity, leadership, deep connection, and accountability. Now, if these inspirational principles were simply left to gather dust, they'd be meaningless and of no use to me or anybody else. Equally, another person may have exactly the same hierarchy of core values as I but attach substantially different meanings to each.

Instead of allowing the interpretation of these principles to remain nebulous, I jotted down my guiding principles to define exactly what those core values mean to me. They are as follows:

- Freedom

  - Protect my freedom of action and embrace choices.

  - Empower others to make conscious decisions.

- Integrity

  - Walk the talk or else don't talk.

- Leadership

  - Lead others to their successes whenever possible.

- Deep Connection

  - Be fully present always.

  - Listen to understand.

- Accountability

  - Take responsibility for successes and failures.

  - Be transparent with decisions.

  - Communicate clearly.

Core values and guiding principles work in tandem to shape our behaviour, which, once it becomes a habit, sets our character. In some cases, you may only need one guiding principle for a core value; in other cases, you may need two or three to illustrate exactly what that value means to you.

For example, if your core value is honesty, then your guiding principles may include always telling the truth, being transparent in communication, and admitting mistakes when you've made them. These guiding principles help hold you accountable to your core value of honesty by making it tangible and actionable.

Now, it's your turn: how do your core values affect what you do every day? How will you know when you are living a life aligned with your core values – what does that look like? If you feel you need to make a course correction, which guiding principles will help get you back on the right path?

The best thing about core values and their associated guiding principles is that the more you live according to your chosen maxims, the easier it will be to stay true to them. Your life will be built around those core values, and you'll attract people who hold similar ones. This in turn builds a tribe that gives you a strong sense of belonging.

Freedom is my highest-ranking core value, and so it has become a fundamental driving force in my business. I naturally attract freedom-loving clients who started their businesses so they could achieve greater independence and explore more options in their lives. Some want to be able to make choices that suit their needs better, some desire the freedom to work in a way that suits them (both in location and work hours), or even prefer to work and live in two different countries as a dual citizen.

Attracting clients that resonate with my core values has had many benefits, two notable ones being that my work is more fulfilling and that my clients and I can build connections easily since we resonate well with each other. My core values have allowed me to attract my tribe, and living your core values will allow you to attract yours.

Your Action:

Define Your Core Values and Guiding Principles – Be the best "you" you can be by staying true to who you are

Though your purpose is like a star that guides you, understanding what qualities you value most will help guide your planning and keep you motivated. Finding, ranking, and living your core values will not only bring you valuable self-knowledge but make you more effective in all areas of your life.

1. Create a list of your values. Use the five exercises in this chapter to list ideals and character traits that are important to you. Write down anything that comes up.

2. Shortlist the five most important values. Identify which values on your list resonate with you the most. These are your core values.

3. Rank your core values in order of importance. Think about situations when two of your core values may not be compatible. Which would you prioritize? Repeat this exercise until you have placed your core values in a hierarchy that makes sense to you.

4. Establish the corresponding guiding principles for each core value. How does each core value look in practice when you are living your life according to that value? Guiding principles take your core value from intangible to something you can easily implement.

CHAPTER 3

LIFE VISION & GOALS – DESIGNING AND BUILDING YOUR FULFILLING LIFE

"When you fail to plan, you plan to fail"

– Anonymous

Have you ever run a marathon? It's a major commitment, just over 42km (26 miles) of unforgiving road. Finishing one is difficult enough even if you choose to walk rather than run the distance. Now, imagine that you are running a marathon without knowing where the finish line is! That is what it's like to not have a vision in life.

Your vision embodies your finish line, your goal, and your destination. It is incredibly helpful to have a clear idea of where it is. Now, imagine that you have a finish line established but no milestones defined. You know where you want to end up, yet nothing gives you any indication that you are heading in the right direction, your lungs burning and calves aching all the while. Even the most disciplined of us can get discouraged and demotivated, let alone lost. Those milestones will not only get us to the finish line but also give us much-needed motivation to forge ahead. We'll talk about setting such milestones in Chapter 4, which covers creating a personal productivity routine.

When you don't have a vision, or just a vague notion like "I want to be rich", you won't even know which way to run when the starting pistol goes off. Before starting a marathon, you'll want to understand exactly where the finish line is and establish milestones along the route so you can plan and track your progress. These milestones, of course, are your shorter-term goals. As you pass one after another, you know that you are on track toward your ultimate vision.

Your vision and the goals along the way can be powerful motivators. Defining these clearly allows you to see how your actions are translating into progress toward the finish line and what you will achieve when you continue to prioritize your vision.

I have seen far too many people embark on their journeys without a finish line or even milestones. At worst, they lose their way completely; at best, they don't progress as fast as they could. My hope is that, by the end of this chapter, you will be able to clearly determine your life vision and the milestones that bring you closer to it.

Establish Your Vision

Vision informs decision-making by giving us a destination we can focus our efforts toward. Our vision defines what makes life feel meaningful, so we can live purposefully and make decisions that help create our thriving life.

A vision is a vivid and aspirational description of a desired future state. It is a mental image of what could be rather than what currently exists.

For your vision to be effective, it needs to be both powerful and evocative. It needs to be vivid so that we are invested in bringing it to life. A vision that feels concrete to us is more impactful. This is why I suggest creating a vision that is a moving picture, not a still image. If you were watching a documentary of your dream life ten years from now, what would that movie look like? The more sharply we can picture our vision, the more emotionally invested we are in making it a reality.

There is a famous story about actor and comedian Jim Carrey. As a visioning exercise, Carrey wrote himself a huge post-dated cheque before he achieved success and became a star. "I wrote myself a cheque for $10 million for 'acting services rendered' and I gave myself 5 years. I dated it Thanksgiving 1995 and I put it in my wallet and I kept it there and it deteriorated and deteriorated. But then, just before Thanksgiving 1995, I found out that I was going to make $10 million on Dumb and Dumber."

This is, of course, a spectacular example of setting your sights high. There's no rule that says you have to be quite as audacious as Carrey. Regardless, your vision needs to be inspiring and get you excited about what lies ahead. That means your vision has to be based on the lifestyle you aspire to having ten years from now, not just what your life will be like if you continue doing things the same old way. When our vision is something that we are excited about and emotionally involved in, we're inspired to make the changes necessary to get there. It pushes us forward and stops us from settling for less because we know the life that – potentially – awaits us.

Most people have some idea of what they want their life to look like in the future, but their desires are too vague to be called a vision. They may want to be financially free at some point or want to grow their business. However, they haven't defined exactly what their ideal life would look like. The starting pistol fires, yet they just wander off, driven by the impulses of the moment instead of a goal they're passionate about.

As a poignant example, one of my clients, Rachel, has a daughter who still has some years left to finish high school. Rachel owns a successful photography business and had some vaguely defined ideas of what she wants to do when her daughter graduated. However, when we started our coaching sessions, she had not thought much about what her ideal life would look like. She was, understandably, focused on the day-to-day operations of her photography business and not looking that far ahead.

Another client, whom we'll call George, knew that he wanted to be financially free in the future. When he came to me for coaching, the income he was drawing from his business only barely covered his lifestyle needs. He was focused on building his business and reinvesting his income, so he wasn't thinking of building his personal nest egg.

We'll come back later to Rachel and George to see how they created their visions and what changes they made to bring them to life. But first, let's have a look at the nuts and bolts of the visioning process.

The Five-Step Visioning Process

I like to break the process of creating a vision down into five steps.

1. Establish Your Baseline: The Wheel of Life Now

2. Establish Your Finish line: The Future Wheel of Life

3. Make Your Vision Holistic

4. Establish Your Leverage & Supporting Goals

5. Turn Your Goals into Actions (the following chapter)

In order to define your vision, you need to start by doing a complete inventory of what your life looks like now.

Step 1: Establish Your Baseline: The Wheel of Life Now

Before you can start making changes, it's important to take stock of what your life is currently like. The Wheel of Life exercise provides a template based on eight aspects of your day-to-day existence so you can assess how fulfilling your life is. You can swap out elements that you feel don't apply in your life for ones that you think are more suitable. It is your situation and your definition of a thriving life that matters in this exercise. If a "significant other" doesn't play a role in your vision, for example, replace it with something else or remove it.

Rate each area of your life out of 10. A rating of 10 means you are fulfilled, and you have everything you could wish for in this area of your life. A rating of 1 signifies that this aspect of your life is far from ideal. I have included some questions below the wheel illustration to help you decide on your score in each area.

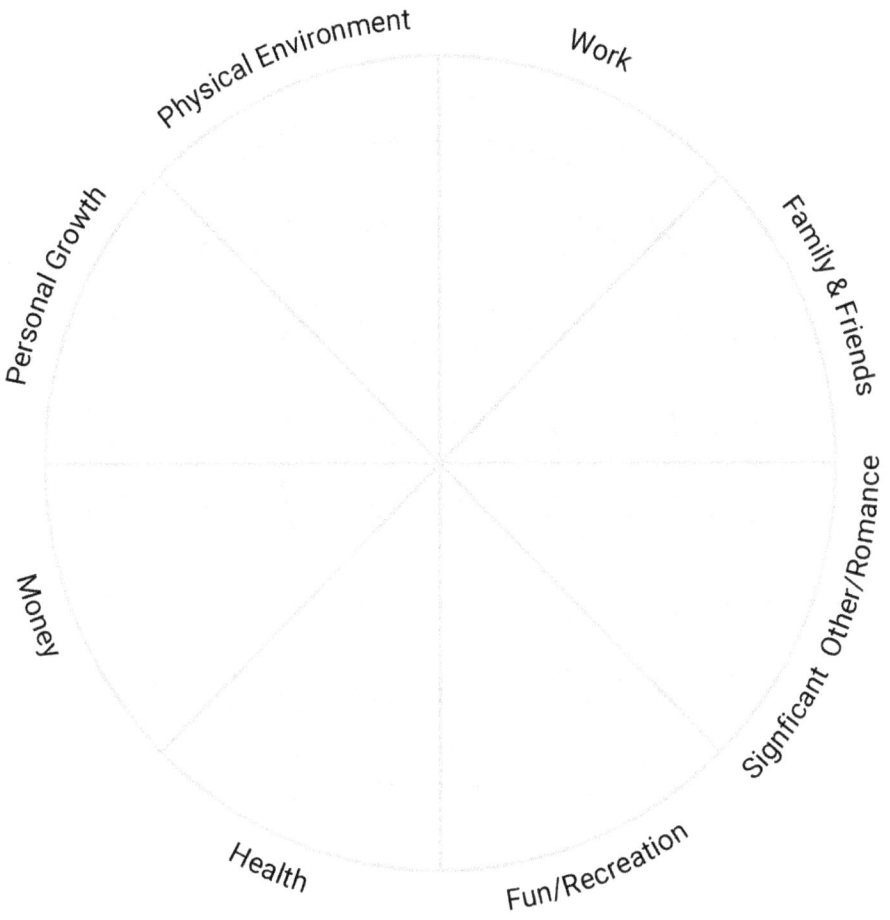

Physical Environment

Work

Personal Growth

Family & Friends

Money

Signficant Other/Romance

Health

Fun/Recreation

<Wheel of Life>

Physical Environment

- How happy are you with your physical environment? Are you happy with your current home? Do you enjoy living or working in your city or country?

- What would make you happier?

- What would make your situation more comfortable?

Work

- How fulfilling is your work right now?

- What does fulfilling work look like to you?

- Are you on a positive path at work?

Family

- How close are you with your family?

- What is missing, if anything, in your relationships with your family?

Relationships/Significant Other

- Do you have a support network that you can lean on?

- How content do you currently feel in your close relationships?

- What would make them better?

Fun and Leisure

- What do you do for fun?

- What do you enjoy doing that you don't do enough of?

Health/Fitness

- Using your personal definition of fitness, how fit are you?

- Are you currently attending to any health concerns?

- Using your definition of a healthy diet, how good are your eating habits?

- Are there improvements to be made?

Money

- Do you feel financially free and secure?

- How satisfied are you with your current level of income?

- How do you feel about your current expenses?

- What impact would financial independence have on your life?

Personal Growth/Spirituality/Fulfillment/Life Purpose

- Do you feel like you are living the life you want, or do you feel like you are living the life someone else wants for you?

- How comfortable do you feel in your own skin?

- Do you have enough "me time"?

This is an easy method of drawing a holistic picture of your current state of fulfillment. You may think you have a pretty good handle on how happy you are in the various aspects of your life, but the results are often surprising! Marking your rankings on the Wheel of Life template gives you a visual representation of how well you're currently doing. It is up to you whether you colour the wheel in or mark the ranking with a line – pick whatever will help you best picture the way things are with you.

Once you've worked through the questions and filled in your Wheel of Life, take a good look at it. What insights does it give you about your circumstances? In which areas of your life are you currently thriving? Celebrate all the ways in which you are fulfilled!

It is important to recognize the areas where you are doing well just as much as identifying segments in which you want to improve. Many of my clients have shared how pleased they were to realize that they were in a better place than they expected. It is so easy to get caught up in finding deficiencies, comparing our lives to those of others, and forgetting to appreciate all the wonderful blessings we already possess. Without doing a structured exercise like the Wheel of Life, we often lose sight of the overall picture because we're focusing on the day-to-day grind. It's very helpful to take stock and be grateful for what you have – celebrate and learn from your current fulfillment!

Looking at the areas where you are most fulfilled, do you see a unifying characteristic? Say you have higher ratings in work, physical environment, and hobbies. You may identify "you have greater control" as a common thread in these. This gives you more information about your current fulfillment and the path to a more satisfying life.

Now that we've celebrated your wins, take a look at where you are currently making compromises. If you're like most of my clients, you may feel compelled to equate the areas with low ratings as "failure". Objectively, this probably isn't true. I encourage you to upgrade your mindset and instead consider these low ratings as opportunities for growth.

This may sound like a counter-intuitive suggestion, but I've seen it work countless times. In fact, one of the productivity habits I suggest to you is that you swap the word "opportunity" for "failure" or "challenge" from this moment on, wherever applicable. Words matter: programming your brain to see opportunity where you formerly perceived defeat will make you so much more dynamic and resourceful.

In aspects where you are currently less fulfilled, what opportunities do you see? Starting a business generally requires a lot of time and energy. We often borrow from other areas of our life to plough more effort into our business. That compromise isn't, or shouldn't be, a permanent state. You probably had really good reasons as to why you made concessions in these areas in the past. What opportunities do you see now to bolster your fulfillment moving forward?

An important philosophical stand I have is that life should be fulfilling now as well as later. While we are creating a long-term vision (the finish line), I believe we should be ambitious enough to create a fulfilling life in the present as well. Eventually pushing through the finish line is great, but the act of running should be enjoyable as well.

The rationale for seeing things this way isn't complicated. I'm not one for delayed gratification. I'm one of those people who will eat my favourite fruit first when it's available, passing over less appetizing options. When a package is delivered to our front door, I open it instantly. Håkan on the other hand, will retrieve it, put it on the foyer table and attend to it later at his convenience.

I will jump at a chance to do something exciting because you never know if that opportunity will arise again. When you get right down to it, we have absolutely no guarantee that the next week, next month, or year will come for us. If you agree with me on this, you'll also agree that no long-term vision is worth building if we have to sacrifice all gratification until we get there. We also need to live in the moment and create our fulfillment for today.

Look at what changes you can make in the next few months to start living a more fulfilling life now and begin scheduling actions toward your goals. (We'll get to some practical advice on doing this in the next chapter.) Even if, at the moment, you can only improve on a couple of things out of a very long list, you can start living more fully today even as you are building your future fulfilling life.

Step 2: Establish Your Finish Line: Future Wheel of Life – The Vision

Choose Your Vision Year

The second step of my visioning process is to come up with a blueprint for the kind of life we want to lead in the future. We'll start by picking a date or event in the future when you hope to achieve your vision. It should be a point that makes sense. Many of my clients pick a major landmark like:

- Milestone birthdays

- When their children graduate from school

- Retirement

These represent times when we are moving into another season in our lives. Pick one that anchors you, like when your youngest child graduates from high school. If nothing obvious comes to mind, choose ten years from now.

If your self-imposed deadline is too close on the horizon, it can be difficult to draw inspiration from it. Your practical brain will try to rein in your vision by thinking about what's possible to achieve based on today's limitations. "What's wrong with being realistic?", you may argue. Well, I say that "realistic" eats "inspiring" for breakfast. Don't limit yourself. More often than not, an inspiring vision is what gets your heart engaged and your mind and actions focused.

Build Your Fulfilling Life

Now that you've set a time in the future for achieving your goals, what would your Wheel of Life look like if you were living your inspiring life? In each of the eight segments of the wheel, how will you be doing and what will you have achieved? Make sure that every one of your goals is aspirational and that they're all in harmony with one another. Take down some notes; you will need to refer to your definition of a thriving life in the next steps.

I'll offer an example to help guide you. One of my clients, Rebecca, is a single mom with a 12-year-old daughter, Emy. When Emy goes to college 6 years from now, Rebecca will be 50 years old. She has the following self-vision for her 50th birthday:

Work: My business is well established, with three boutique operations, and sustainable with a strong team of managers in each branch. I am not involved in daily operations anymore and instead spend my time supporting my branch managers who run the day-to-day. I work 15 hours a week and only get involved in business development and strategic oversight. I spend the rest of my time volunteering for various local organizations, helping kids.

Money: Each branch is netting $5,000 per month on average, and I've automatically invested $5k each month under my business name and made another $5k in personal investments for the past six years.

Health/Well-being: I have established an exercise regime (three times a week) and walk every day for at least half an hour – sometimes with friends and colleagues.

Physical environment: I have downsized to an apartment (one bedroom + den), as Emy has moved out. I have a very quiet office space that allows for productive virtual meetings with my managers when I don't have to go into the branches. It's a minimalist environment with a lot of white space.

Hobby/Recreation: I travel abroad for fun – often with one of my good friends – and combine these trips with volunteer work whenever I can.

Family and Friends: I have a few friends I care for deeply. I regularly meet up with them (once or twice a week) and genuinely connect with them. I remain close with my brother and his family and keep in regular contact with my mum, even though they live in different countries. My daughter Emy and I are as close as any mom and daughter could hope to be. We are like best friends.

Overall, future Rebecca is content with her life. Over the years, she has learned to focus on what matters truly in life, rather than what's pushed in front of her by others. She is in charge of where she's going. What is your finish line?

It's time for you to draw an ambitious and inspiring holistic life success vision. Make it as detailed as you can. Once you have chosen the year, place yourself in that timeframe and write in the present tense, like Rebecca did, as if you have achieved your vision fully. Engage all three parts of your awareness – your head (rational and problem-solving), your heart (passion and feelings), and your gut (intuition and courage).

Step 3: Make Your Vision Holistic

How will you know when you've created a credible, audacious, and balanced vision? There are three elements essential to any effective vision, or any major life plan for that matter. As a statement of purpose, your vision must be:

- **Inspiring:** You must be excited about your vision so that you are motivated to make the changes necessary to make it a reality.

- **Holistic:** Your vision must help you thrive in all areas of your life. Prioritizing finances over family, for example, is something you can do only temporarily. Instead, try to find a way to make these two aspects of your ideal life work in harmony.

- **Attainable:** Your vision must be achievable, assuming you consistently devote the right amount of time and energy.

In this part of the visioning process, we will challenge your vision until it meets all three of those criteria. Your first draft doesn't have to be carved in stone; allow your imagination and self-awareness free rein, and don't be afraid of refining your chosen aspirations.

Let's start by mentally playing the documentary of your future life. (Imagining that you've achieved everything that's important to you and working backward from there may not seem like an obvious way to plan, but it does work. Computer programmers often use this technique, asking themselves: "Assuming that the problem has just been solved, what would have been the previous step?" You'll encounter the same technique in Chapter 9.) Is your biography inspiring? Do you sense your heart filled with joy and happiness as you watch your progress through your journey? Do you feel pride and fulfillment? How does each element of your life relate to the others?

These are hard questions to answer. Take your time. Interrogate your goals until they work together as a holistic vision. You will probably want to revise some of your vision's elements if these conflict with the rest of the wheel. Consider the real motivation for your goals. You can do this over several days and make a little U-turn now and then; that's okay.

Let's say Paul has a vision for the life he wants to lead in ten years' time. He wants to be a supportive and caring parent and partner. He wants to work part-time in the business he owns and have a large vegetable garden on his own property. Sounds simple when you condense it like that, doesn't it?

In reality, this vision addresses multiple aspects of his Wheel of Life. He follows a healthy lifestyle, by his own standards, because he eats a plant-based diet and most of his food is harvested fresh from his own garden. He has a small but highly dedicated core team of employees who have made it easy for him to remove himself from the day-to-day operations of his company. Now, he is only needed for business development, amounting to 10 to 15 hours per week. The rest of his time is spent working on his garden, hanging out with family and friends, and volunteering at the local food bank.

This is an effective vision. Let's reflect back on the essential prereq- uisites: it is holistic, inspiring, and achievable. We can see that each of these elements supports the others. The vision is also vivid. Paul can easily picture how he would spend the average day or week in his future life, so he becomes emotionally invested in it. And everything he specified can be achieved through consistent progress within a 10-year timeframe. This is a winning vision.

Let's look at an alternative to the same vision. It starts the same: Paul's friend Peter also wants to be a supportive parent and partner. So far, so good. By Peter's definition, that means being present for the important events in his family's lives. However, he also wants to expand his business and take his operations international. Specifically, he wants branches on three continents within the next ten years. He also wants to own a house in Vancouver and a few investment properties. He wishes to be healthy and happy, too.

All of the above are things most of us may aspire to. Yet, there's some- thing wrong. When it comes to picturing this second example as a doc- umentary, we run into some difficulties. This vision requires Peter to be everywhere at once. Unlike Paul in the first example, Peter will most likely have to travel regularly in order to run operations on three continents. That will get in the way of being present in the lives of his loved ones. There will need to be some prioritization. So, which is more important?

In terms of health, for example, busy executives can live a healthy lifestyle; however, it will be more difficult for Peter than it is for Paul in the first example. How will Peter achieve both physical wellness and com- mercial success?

The problem is that Peter's vision is not holistic yet. Compromises would need to be made in favour of certain elements in his life, disparaging others. He needs to make adjustments now in order to avoid these conflicts.

We can look at all of the elements in Peter's vision and try to find true, worthy motivations for the goals in each sector of his Wheel of Life. You need to make sure these are in harmony, though, or your worst enemy will be yourself. For example, Peter can look at the true purpose behind his desire for international expansion. In order to get to our real motivation, try what I call "the Russian doll" exercise. Here is how it works:

What would international expansion to three continents give me?
Global reputation.

What would a global reputation give me?
More clients.

What would more clients give me?
More money.

What would more money give me?
I'll be rich sooner.

What would being rich sooner give me?
Quality of life for my family.

What would quality of life for my family give me?
Happiness.

Unless you take active responsibility for defining your purpose in life, you'll be lost and confused when the starting pistol goes off. The marathon in front of you is long: it helps to know that you're at least running in the right direction.

Continue this exercise until you're completely satisfied with the result; I promise you that this is time well spent. Then ask yourself: "Can I achieve this quality of life and happiness in other ways than a three-continent global expansion while also creating life success in a holistic sense?" (Or, whatever may be appropriate to your vision.) You bet you can! To illustrate how this can be done, let's return to Rachel's vision.

Once Rachel and I sat down and thought about her vision, she realized that by the time she turns 57, her child will just have graduated from high school. At that point, she wants to live in an eco-village in Costa Rica during part of the year. Her photography studios would still be providing her with sufficient income to cover her lifestyle needs, but she would not need to be involved in their daily operations. She would have established a strong leadership team that she trusted to run things for her. She would spend her time volunteering, travelling, and visiting loved ones.

Note how this is a holistic vision: each of the elements supports the others. She has identified how she will make it possible to work part-time in her business and what her additional free time will enable her to do.

Step 4: Establish One Leverage Goal and One Supporting Goal

What we'll do next is to choose one leverage goal and one supporting goal to focus our efforts. This is an efficient way to actualize your vision without getting overwhelmed by trying to progress in all areas at once.

The leverage goal is the cornerstone of the vision; a practical achievement that makes everything else possible. What is the key accomplishment that all the goals of our vision hinge upon? For Rachel, that element is having a strong leadership team for her business. Without this, she won't be able to take a step back from the day-to-day operations nor will she be able to open three additional studios. Her primary goal and the focus of her efforts, therefore, is to identify and train a general manager to run the businesses. Having this leverage goal in place helps make her decisions clearer. For instance, her chosen manager joined in leadership coaching with me and gradually assumed more and more responsibility.

What's your leverage goal? Which aspect of your vision would bring you significantly closer to achieving all your interlinked long-term goals? For many of my clients, this is a business goal because their enterprise supports their lifestyle. For Rachel, it was establishing strong leadership for her studios. Developing potential leaders in her business is, in effect, a way to help her achieve her ideal lifestyle.

For George, who you may remember from earlier in the chapter, his leverage goal was to grow his business to a certain size. This would allow him to draw more income from it and thereby achieve his personal goals. While we were working on his vision, he realized he hadn't even begun building a personal nest egg, even though financial freedom was a cornerstone of his plans for the future.

Without a clear vision, there was no blueprint to help him construct his ideal life. Now that George has a clear vision, he is putting more money into his retirement savings and saving to purchase his first home. He also knows just how much cash his business needs to generate for him to afford his lifestyle needs, both now and later.

Once you have your leverage goal firmly in mind, it is time to choose a supporting goal that reinforces your vision. The idea here is to reduce the likelihood of things going awry. Think about which segment of the Wheel of Life is most likely to sabotage your success across all elements.

This could be your health and wellness. An injury or illness would impact your ability to achieve all elements of your vision. For many of my clients, including Rachel and George, their businesses are their families' main source of income. If they were no longer able to work, it would impact their ability to achieve their holistic vision, not to mention their family's welfare.

Family is another common supporting goal. A disharmonious relationship with those closest to you has the potential to distract you from your business. If your interactions with some family members are a source of stress rather than support, these bonds need to be addressed in some way to help you achieve your vision. This may mean resolving some long-standing conflict so you can move forward. In some cases, the best course of action may be to deprioritize that relationship so it is not an ever-present stressor.

Step 5: Turn Your Goals into Actions

The final step of the visioning process is to turn your leverage goal and supporting goals into actions, scheduled in your calendar. We will look at this step in more detail in the next chapter. For now, just keep in mind that an abstract vision, by itself, doesn't achieve anything.

Once you've defined your vision, leverage goal, and supporting goal, let's move on to the next chapter to create your productivity routine.

Your Action:

Define Your Vision and Establish Your Leverage and Supporting Goal–Set a clear finish line for your journey and define the major milestones that will help you get there.

Now it's time for you to put the visioning exercise into practice, if you haven't already. Referring back to the examples in this chapter, set aside a decent amount of time to spend by yourself and complete the following checklist:

1. Fill out your current Wheel of Life. How fulfilling is the existence you enjoy right now? Remember: you can swap out elements to better cover the aspects of life that are important to you.

2. Envision your future Wheel of Life. What would it look like if you were thriving across all these areas?

    a) Which year are you creating your vision for?

    b) What constitutes your thriving life? Use the elements in the template as a guide.

3. Review your vision to make sure it is:

    a) Inspiring – You must be excited about your vision and motivated to make the changes necessary to turn it into reality.

    b) Holistic – Your vision must help you thrive in all areas of your life, with each element supporting the others.

    c) Attainable – Your vision must be within reach if you consistently devote your time and energy to achieving your goals.

4. Determine your leverage and supporting goals. Which two elements can you focus on to make significant progress toward your vision (leverage goal) and minimize the risk of failure (supporting goal)?

5. Write all of this down in a place where you can easily refer to it. You will need to review your vision often. I use the tool SmartArt to keep all elements of my vision in one place.

CHAPTER 4

YOUR PRODUCTIVITY SYSTEM – YOUR PERSONAL METHOD TO ACTUALIZE YOUR VISION AND GOALS

"Sow a thought, and you reap an act;
Sow an act, and you reap a habit;
Sow a habit, and you reap a character;
Sow a character, and you reap a destiny."

— Samuel Smiles, Author of "Happy Homes
and the Hearts That Make Them"

Identifying the Roots of Your Challenges

In 2012, Google partnered with researchers at Yale and St. Joseph's University to examine the eating habits of staff at Google. It had become commonplace for Google employees to gain weight during their first six months with the company. New hires were actually warned about the "Google 15" – the number of pounds they could expect to put on – during their induction. Realizing that offering free food as a perk had produced unintended consequences, Google looked for ways it could induce its employees to follow healthier lifestyles.

Researchers from Yale spent time in Google's break rooms and micro-kitchens, discreetly observing employee behaviour. These micro-kitchens all had different layouts, and the researchers noticed that the floor plans had a significant impact on employees' habits. In one micro-kitchen, where the snack bar was 6.5ft from the coffee brewing station and drink fridge, employees were 50% more likely to grab a snack than in another, where snacks were displayed 17.5ft away. In a 2016 paper, the research team noted simply that people tend to eat more when food is easy to see and reach. They suggested that nothing but convenience was leading to higher rates of snacking among Google employees.

While Google can't force its staff to go to the gym or dictate what food they eat, it focused on what it could control – the environment employees worked in. Yale professor Ravi Dhar described the changes Google made as shuffling the alternatives, not changing them. "They kept all of their snack and beverage options but just rearranged them."

This example highlights something that is at the heart of my coaching strategy surrounding productivity routines. Willpower alone isn't always enough. We can't count on ourselves to make choices that support our goals 100% of the time. What we can do is take a cue from Google and curate our environment so that it is easier to make decisions in line with our vision.

Curating our environment to change our behaviour is a concept emphasized in the book "Atomic Habits" by James Clear. Here are a few reasons, as mentioned in the book, why it is important to curate our environment:

Make desired behaviours obvious: When cues for desired behaviour are visible in our environment, they serve as reminders and prompt us to take action. For example, if you want to exercise more, laying out your workout clothes and keeping your running shoes by the door can make it easier to exercise more consistently.

Reduce friction for positive habits: Similarly, we should look to reduce the barriers or obstacles to our desired behaviours. For instance, if you want to spend less time on social media, you can delete distracting apps from your phone or use website blockers to limit access during certain hours. When my partner Håkan and I watch a movie or news in the evenings, we prepare and lay out carrot sticks, nuts, and other healthy snacks on our coffee table. This automatically reduces the odds of one of us getting the idea to open a bag of potato chips, cheese puffs, or some other form of empty calories. Chances of Håkan peeling carrots or prepping orange wedges mid-movie are, let's be honest, not very high. Simply making it easier to do the right things – reducing friction – is a great way to encourage positive habits.

Optimize for success: Curating our environment allows us to upgrade it in a way that supports progress and aligns our space with our goals. This, along with developing positive habits, is precisely what we intend to do in this chapter. By designing our environment to include more cues for desired behaviours, we make it easier to actualize our vision and goals.

This productivity system builds on the work you have been doing so far to build the foundation of a fulfilling life, both now and in the future. Without it, your ambitious goals can get lost in the daily grind. It's far too easy to tell yourself you will work on the truly important stuff later, when you have "more time" or after your "busy season". The problem is: "later" never materializes. This happens despite how much you want to achieve your vision and goals. Challenges abound in actualizing our vision. No wonder so many of us basically sleepwalk through our entire life journey. Desire is not the problem; the problem is lacking a productivity system that ensures that our focus is always on our vision.

Once we've worked out our vision and milestones, we need to optimize our environment to reduce friction and avoid losing our way amid the daily bustle. The best way I have found to do that is to create a productivity system that prioritizes regular action towards our goals.

First, though, take a moment to think of simple ways to better curate your environment. These could be as straightforward as getting a more ergonomic pillow, preparing a week's meals in advance every Sunday to save time later, or installing a time management app on your computer.

The Solution: Your Productivity System

A common misconception about productivity is that it measures the number of tasks you can accomplish in a day. Doing more with your time can certainly be helpful, but it can also become an excuse for essentially running in place and avoiding important, yet intimidating, responsibilities. This means you're constantly busy but not necessarily accomplishing much. My definition of productivity focuses instead on the actions that truly move your vision forward. Seen from this perspective, productivity is the ability to identify what tasks you need to complete, prioritize them based on their importance, and then dedicate the time and energy needed to complete them in an efficient manner.

In other words, productivity means accomplishing the things that matter to you. The most important of these are encapsulated in your vision, your leverage and supporting goals. The following five steps will help you create your personal productivity system:

1. Focus on your vision, along with your leverage goal and supporting goal, as a guide.
2. Establish S.M.A.R.T. goals.
3. Build routines into your calendar.
4. Break down your SMART goals into actions, then schedule them in your calendar.
5. Stay on course using your schedule.

Let's return to Rebecca's example to illustrate how to use these steps in practice.

As you may recall, Rebecca is a single mom with a 12-year-old daughter, Emy. When Emy goes to college 6 years from now, Rebecca will be 50 years old. Let's recap her self-vision for that occasion:

Work: Her business is well established, comprising three boutique operations, and sustainable with a strong leadership team running each branch. She is not involved in daily operations anymore and instead supports her branch managers, who are in charge of the day-to-day decisions. She works 15 hours per week and only gets involved in business development and providing strategic direction. She spends the rest of her time volunteering for various local organizations dedicated to helping kids.

Money: Each branch is yielding an average monthly net of $5000, and she has been automatically investing 5K a month under her business's name and made another 5K in monthly personal investments for the past six years.

Health/Well-being: She has established her exercise regime (three times a week) and walks every day for at least half an hour – sometimes with some of her friends and colleagues.

Physical Environment: She has now downsized to a one-bedroom + den apartment, as Emy has moved out. She has a very quiet office space that allows for productive virtual meetings with her managers if she doesn't need to visit the branches. It's a minimalist environment with few distractions and a lot of white space.

Hobby/Recreation: Rebecca often travels abroad for fun – sometimes with one of her good friends – and combines these trips with volunteering for different organizations whenever she can.

Family and Friends: She has a few close friends she deeply cares for. She meets them once or twice a week and connects deeply with them. Rebecca is close to her brother and his family, and she keeps in regular contact with her mother even though they live in different countries. Rebecca and Emy are as close as any mom and daughter could hope to be. They are like best friends.

Overall, Rebecca is content with her life. Over the years, she has learned to focus on what truly matters in life rather than what others tell her is important. Now, let's see how she converted her vision into an action plan and a productivity system:

1. Focus on Your Vision, Along with Your Leverage Goal and Supporting Goal, as a Guide

It's now time to revisit your vision, as well as the leverage goal and supporting goal you established to guide you toward it. We're going to turn these goals into actions that you can start working on today.

Rebecca's leverage goal is to have three branches of her business established and running smoothly. This enables the rest of the vision – a steady income of 5k per location for her lifestyle needs as well as investments.

Her supporting goal is health, as a lack of physical vigour will sabotage her leverage goal and cause a domino effect, jeopardizing the rest of her vision.

2. Establish S.M.A.R.T. Goals

Now that you have your vision, leverage and supporting goals firmly in mind, the next step is to create SMART milestones on the way to achieving those goals. I've added a couple of examples just to illustrate the process. But first, a little information about SMART, a system that's universally recognized as a powerful tool in the business world:

Specific (S): Goals must be clear and unambiguous. Does your goal answer the questions of who, what, where, when, why, and how? The more specific your goal is, the easier it is to work towards.

Measurable (M): Goals need to have concrete and clear criteria you can use to measure your progress and success. These include dates, numbers, percentages, and metrics. Establish your criteria from the very start, or it may not be obvious whether you've accomplished a certain goal.

Achievable (A): Goals must be realistic and feasible, yet challenging enough to inspire growth. Can you achieve your goal with focused efforts? Consider your available resources, skills, and time when setting goals.

Relevant (R): Goals need to align with your personal and business aspirations and priorities. They should have a meaningful impact on your personal and professional growth and bring you closer to achieving your vision.

Timebound (T): Goals must have a specific timeline or deadline. By setting a target timeframe, you create a sense of urgency and establish accountability. Having a deadline also helps with prioritization and planning.

Rebecca's 3-year SMART goals for her leverage goal are:

- Establish a new business plan to accomplish the expansion by *mid-year.*

- Assemble a board to support her expansion plans and branch management by the *end of the year.*

For her supporting goal (Health & Well-Being):

- Establish an exercise routine in her calendar *by the end of this week.*

- Develop a training programme, using YouTube videos, *by the end of the month.*

- Establish a consistent 30-minute lunch break habit *by this Sunday.*

Note how each of these goals meets the SMART criteria. At this point, when you have a moment to yourself, refer back to your holistic vision of success in life and look at what is important. What additional planning needs to be done to allow you to progress in the areas you've identified? Incorporate these into your calendar, in addition to SMART-based actions towards your leverage goal and supporting goal – we'll get to the procedure for doing so in just a moment.

First, though, I'd like to reiterate that our object here is to build a framework for our productivity system. Willpower and good intentions, while certainly positive attributes, aren't always enough. It is only once we structure our lives according to our vision that we access the self-discipline necessary to make consistent progress toward our goals.

3. Build Routines into Your Calendar – Make Appointments with Yourself

If your SMART milestones on the way to achieving your leverage and support goals are sufficiently challenging, it's a fair bet that you won't achieve them by accident or by following the same old habits. What routines can you create that will help you to steadily build your ideal life? Rebecca has already identified two routines for her productivity (meaning: focusing on the stuff that matters), namely her exercise and lunch break schedule. She uses her digital calendar to set up recurring appointments with herself for those two routines.

In addition to building your SMART goals into your calendar, it can be helpful to create a daily, weekly, and monthly routine that allows you to make regular progress toward your targets. What routines would you benefit from if they became daily habits? How will they end up boosting your progress towards your vision and goals? A while back, Håkan and I established our morning ritual, starting with meditation, then gratitude, before making the bed. Once I'm at my desk after breakfast, I start my workday by bringing up "Calendar View" in MS Outlook and take some time to plan the day's activities. This sets me up for a day where I'm sure of getting things done.

This forms part of my productivity system; yours will most likely be different. What routine will help you to make each day productive? What routines will help you to build a productive week, month, or year?

I strongly suggest that you establish a planning/development routine in your calendar as soon as possible. This turns you from a reactive person to a proactive one. On Monday mornings, I spend 30 minutes to two hours organizing and refining my blueprint for the future, both near and distant. I do my best to ensure that I'll have no interruptions while doing this, so I can devote my full attention to identifying opportunities and finding ways of relieving bottlenecks. This dedicated occasion has become a fixed part of my routine, just like meditation and exercise. I use that time to plan my week, review my monthly goals, and look further ahead to my long-term agenda and vision.

Scheduling development and planning time is an essential routine any business leader should include in their schedule. It allows you to keep in regular touch with your goals and vision, so that your priorities aren't neglected due to the turbulence of day-to-day life. Planning also allows you to make timely adjustments so that small concerns don't become urgent problems due to neglect and inattention.

How frequently do you currently check up on your performance and progress? This may take the form of weekly sales analyses, monthly expense audits, quarterly vision and goal reviews, and so on. These should now go into your calendar as a recurring appointment with yourself – this routine will serve you well. Don't consider this a paper exercise, either. As I often say to my coaching clients, take the meetings that you make with yourself seriously. Those are the ones that will get you the biggest dividend from your investment of time.

I'm sharing part of my routine schedule as a sample below.

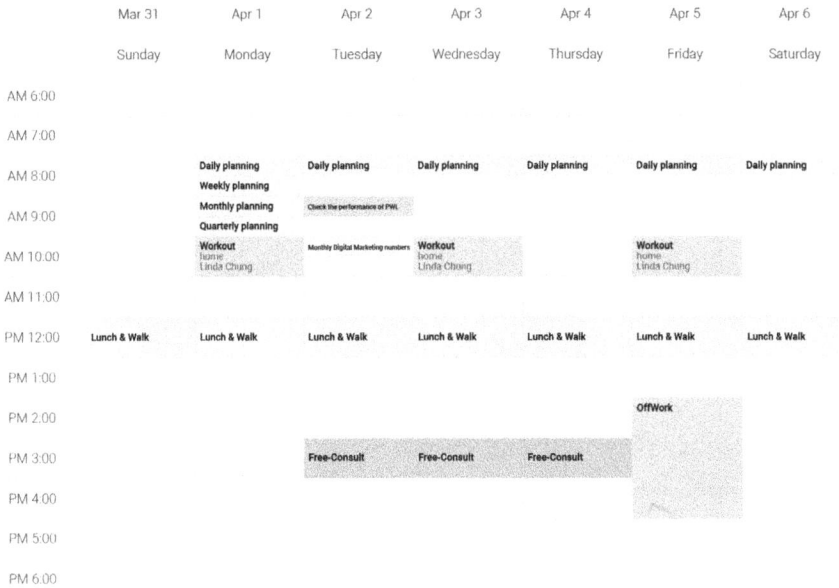

<Sample Productivity Routine>

As you can see, I have my planning sessions scheduled ahead of time, making it difficult to ignore them. Outlook supports adding recurring appointments, so it is easy to put these sessions in your schedule as regular events. I also use Monday as my business development day, so I can prioritize working on my company.

In my case, ongoing professional development is important not only for my own fulfillment, based on delivering high-quality services, but also for maintaining my ICF credentials. I spend Mondays on professional as well as business development. Those two activities don't usually take up the whole day, but making them the focus of my Mondays ensures that I'm always on top of things.

One of my clients, Mark, aspires to be a leader in his industry instead of just chasing after trends. In addition to planning ahead, he schedules a dedicated time every week to actively pursue information related to his field and subsequently create strategies to take advantage of new developments. By scheduling time to read and assiduously broadening his knowledge, he puts himself in a position to be a trailblazer, because he is well-equipped to spot emerging trends. He has also identified the industry heavyweights that he wants to work with and puts regular catch-ups with them in his schedule.

As you can see in my schedule above, I always include a daily lunch and walk break between 12 and 1, plus three weekly home workout sessions to bolster my fitness, overall health, and vitality. Looking at the general direction of my schedule items, you may be able to detect my life purpose of "helping people live fulfilling lives". For instance, I set up three free consulting sessions each week. I place a lot of stock in being generous with my expertise. I also leave work for the week right after lunch on Fridays. This is a deliberate decision to preserve my lifestyle and my free time.

Remember that "fun and leisure" also make up a segment on the Wheel of Life. Even if your supporting goal doesn't directly touch on this aspect, it's important to schedule time for rest and recreation. No matter how ambitious and dedicated you are, it's difficult to operate at your full potential if you're constantly stressed and exhausted.

Let's take a moment to think about what is important in your life. How can you prioritize these items in your calendar? Some of my clients have explicitly set aside 6 to 9 p.m. every evening as their family time. This may seem unnecessary; perhaps your core values are somewhat different from theirs. However, they made this decision after they found themselves devoting so many hours to business that they were allowing it to creep into the time they'd rather spend with their loved ones. Now, they've re-prioritized their families, reframed this as a routine, and are far happier overall.

Your time should be organized around your routine, not the other way around. Your calendar, not the whims of the moment, should determine how you spend your day. When you follow a defined schedule, you don't wait for a free moment to attend to the most important tasks. In this way, you ensure that the SMART goals that mark the path to your fulfilling life are prioritized. You'll be able to ensure these are given the first pick of your attention and energy. Remember: what you focus on grows. Make sure that you grow the right things.

Everybody's ideal schedule will look different, but you do need to create a productivity routine that supports your fulfilling life. This will require a little bit of trial and error at first; experiment here and there and make a note of what works. I touch base with my clients every so often about their productivity routine as well as their leverage goal and supporting goal. After all, if a coach isn't an accountability partner, she is neglecting a major part of coaching. This helps my clients stay on track. If they've missed their lunchtime walk, I ask them: "What is making it so difficult to take that break?" From there, we discuss solutions and/or adjustments to their schedule.

If you have a spouse or close friend to bounce productivity ideas and thoughts about your SMART goals off, so much the better. You may even search out a life or business coach to help optimize your productivity system. I may be slightly biased in this regard, but only because I've seen how professional coaching has benefited numerous people. Having an accountability partner is like buying an insurance policy for achieving your goals.

If your established schedule isn't working for you, ask yourself: "What is getting in the way of me staying on track?" Once you've identified what's holding you back, ask: "In similar circumstances previously, what strategies worked well for me?"

Now, go ahead and establish your planning routine.

- Determine your calendar platform for all of your activities, personal and business. I like Microsoft Outlook, Google Calendar offers a cloud-based option, while there are more mobile scheduling apps than you can shake a stick at.

- Schedule your daily, weekly, and monthly planning sessions. Dedicate this time to tracking your progress towards your leverage and supporting goals, and programming your future actions.

- Are there any elements of your vision that you want to incorporate into your routine on a daily, weekly, monthly, and yearly basis? Go ahead and make a recurring appointment with yourself.

4. Break Down Your SMART Goals into Actions, then Schedule Them in Your Calendar

We've already covered the importance of establishing productive routines. Your SMART goals, too, should be added to your calendar, once you've dissected them into smaller tasks.

For example, one of Rebecca's SMART goals is to establish a new business plan for her expansion. That is a huge, intimidating project, so she breaks it down into smaller milestones. Here are some of the tasks she might schedule into her calendar:

- Carve out half an hour first thing in the morning every day for the next 2 weeks to work on my business plan.

- Brainstorm the process with my coach. Ask for an existing template.

- Create a weekly leadership meeting to brainstorm/develop a business plan.

Considering your available time and resources, and your leverage and supporting goals, what kind of actionable tasks can you decide on? Now, schedule the actions that will help you achieve your SMART goals in your calendar.

Rebecca decides that she will use 7:30-8:00 AM as her quiet time to work on the plan and puts in a recurring daily commitment in her calendar for two weeks. It's such a simple step, but a great way to get on the right track.

She then uses part of this half-hour on the first day to write an email to her coach and shares her desire to talk about her plans at her next coaching session.

She sends out a recurring weekly meeting scheduled with her leadership team in for the coming month, along with an agenda and notes on the direction she foresees for her business.

5. Stay on Course – The Schedule

There is a saying about the best-laid plans... You can certainly expect a few setbacks along the way; after all, the whole point of having a supporting goal is to avoid or minimize the worst of these. You are in greater control than you probably realize, though. However, the success of your productivity system all hinges on you sticking to your own schedule.

If Rebecca ignores her calendar, there would be no actualization of her vision. She may as well not have a schedule at all for all the good it does her.

You could be sitting on top of a gold mine, yet you won't see any rewards unless you start digging for the gold.

I often finish my coaching sessions with, "Don't be busy. Be productive!" When your focus is on the right thing – your vision, your core values, and your goals – your daily energy will be directed at it. The key to making things happen is through following your schedule, culminating in establishing your productivity system. Your chance of living your fulfillment is far greater when you are working according to a schedule which emphasizes productivity: taking care of the things that truly matter.

Habits as Your Aid for Productivity, Routines as Your Productivity System

"Repetition rewires the brain and breeds habits. When neurons fire together often, they begin to fire together at a quicker rate."

– John B. Arden, Psychologist

Many of my clients have health as a supporting goal because their business operations rely on their constant involvement. If an unexpected health issue forced them to take time off, it would negatively impact their business and therefore their livelihood. Depending on how long they had to spend recovering, an illness might also delay their goals and vision coming to fruition. So, respecting their supporting goal, my clients often set regular, scheduled habits around exercise and nutrition.

When we first start making these kinds of changes, they are often so small that they seem absurd or pointless. If you are starting from zero or if you need to undo some bad habits first, a gradual approach is probably best. Some of my clients are leading sedentary lifestyles when they begin exploring their vision, core values, and goals. They sometimes chuckle when I suggest that they start by putting out their running shoes where they are clearly visible. However minor this action appears, though, what we are doing is creating an environment that is conducive to the habit we are trying to create. Just like Google did with its employees, we are trying to reduce the friction to taking our desired action and make it more difficult to take the option that works against our goals.

The human body is biologically lazy: it is conditioned to conserve energy. The same is true of our minds. When given a choice, we are more likely to take the path of least resistance, mentally and physically. This may be a depressing concept, but you can also make it work in your favour. For instance, we tend to think twice about grabbing a snack if we have to walk all the way to the kitchen to reach it. Not applying this principle means our body won't want to work out; we need to make exercising the path of least resistance instead. Taking a hard look at where you are and where you're going can be uncomfortable; scheduling regular, non-negotiable sessions for planning and tracking your progress makes it easier.

This lesson is pretty much intuitive once you think about it. I use this knowledge in my own life. Monday, Wednesday, and Friday mornings, first thing before breakfast, I set up my yoga mat and weights in the living room and put my sneakers in the middle of the yoga mat. If I don't want to work out, then I still need to put everything away, so skipping my workout is no longer such an easy option. If I end up putting them away without working out, I will also have to face my guilty conscience. Working out becomes the easier option.

Making your habits consistent fixtures in your schedule is another way to create an environment conducive to your goals. After a few weeks of following your new routine, you'll notice that the people around you know that Monday mornings are your business planning time or you go to the gym between 12 and 1 every day. It becomes routine for them too, and that supports your productivity system. Your staff won't book meetings or try to contact you during that time. Your family will steer clear of the living room during your regular workout session. Supporting your routine becomes their routine.

Your Action:

Build Your Productivity System and Take it Seriously – Own your routines and ensure that they're helping you achieve your SMART goals.

Structuring your time is essential to staying productive and organized. A productivity system is not about getting more done in less time, it's about focusing your time, energy, and effort on the important stuff. By creating routines around your desired results and outcomes, it is easier to make consistent progress towards your goals.

Complete the five steps to create your productivity routines and system now:

1. Refer back to your Wheel of Life, vision, and your leverage and supporting goals – these dictate the first things we'll be putting in your calendar.

2. Establish SMART goals toward your leverage and supporting goals – What are some things you can do in the immediate future to take the first steps towards these achievements? Set SMART (Specific, Measurable, Attainable, Relevant, and Timebound) milestones around them and schedule them in your calendar.

3. Establish routines in your calendar to support your vision and goals:

   a) Turn your leverage and supporting goals into small daily or weekly actions and schedule them. Some will be regular appointments with yourself, others milestones on the way to achieving your SMART goals.

   b) Choose when you want to do your daily and weekly business planning and put this routine into your schedule, too. Set a recurring calendar entry for this so you are forced to organize everything else around these tasks.

4. Break down your SMART goals into actions – Finally, dissect your smart goals into individual, actionable tasks and schedule them into your calendar. Your brain will want to take the path of

least resistance, so it will follow the schedule rather than having to find something else to do.

5. Stay on course – Follow your schedule and make adjustments as needed to overcome friction or increase your progress.

PART II

SCALE YOUR BUSINESS: BUILD TO THRIVE

"To reach a port we must set sail – sail, not tie at anchor; sail, not drift."

– Franklin D. Roosevelt

Chapter 5: Core Strengths–Your Value Propositions to Your Clients, Your Employees, and the World

Chapter 6: Core Purpose–Your Gift to the World: Your Business's "Why", Your Cause, and the Common Thread that Ties Your Stakeholders to Your Company

Chapter 7: Core Values & Guiding Principles– The Culture and Glue of Your Tribe and a Guide on How to Build a Unified Crew

Chapter 8: Core Focus - Your Specialization–Your Reputation and Irresistible Offer

Chapter 9: Launching Your Ambitious Vision– The Driver and Focus of All Things in Your Business, Your Collective Dreams and Goals

Chapter 10: Leading Others with Empowerment– Pulling Together Towards Your Vision

Chapter 11: Designing Your Elite Team– Work in Unison to Deliver Your Vision

In Part I, we discussed self-leadership. Returning to the metaphor of the small boat, the rower must know the purpose and destination of the journey, as well as possess the necessary navigational skills and tools needed to complete it efficiently. This is exactly what we covered in Part I. You now know what makes a productive leader: a clear life purpose, vision, and core values, all backed up by an efficient productivity system. Now that you are ready to take on an ambitious journey, it is time to prepare the boat. Do you have a vessel that will get you to your destination? In this section, we will look at preparing and building your productive business.

I have seen countless business leaders who work very hard yet find themselves in the same conundrum over and over. They lament about how ever-elusive business success is. Some wins provide them with hope, but then the next challenge comes along and once again batters their self-confidence. Every company, of course, can experience difficulties with employees, or an economic downturn, or a shift in the market, at any time. Events like these can easily leave us feeling demotivated and unsure of ourselves. Perhaps you started your business in order to gain more freedom and live your ideal lifestyle; now, you wonder what happened to that dream.

It is time to ask if our boat is well-built, watertight, and suited to navigate the waters we will be crossing. Another, related question is: "Do we have the right crew for the journey?"

Part II of this book will provide you with a blueprint to build your vessel – not a generic rowboat nor even necessarily a luxury yacht. Instead, it will be an effective, appropriate boat designed and built specifically for your destination. Here is the thing: what use will the world's most powerful motorboat be to you if your goal is just to get to the next anchorage and enjoy the scenery along the way?

Have you ever seen sports cars in a crowded city travelling at 10 km an hour from one stoplight to the next? They always do that "rev" thing while stuck in traffic, as if to say: "Look how (unnecessarily) powerful I am", then speed off instantly at the green light only to have to brake again a few seconds later. At the end of the day, they still have to comply with the law and yield to the realities of city traffic. More often than not, they're a source of amusement for their fellow drivers.

Sailing in a boat which is not tailored to your needs is a little like driving a Ferrari in central Vancouver. Setting out in an unsuitable vessel is very likely to waste your energy and make your business venture unproductive. Constructing the wrong kind of boat swallows lots of input and may result in very small gains. If it is bigger than you need, it is likely to cost you a lot more money, plus more time and energy to build. Conversely, a boat that's too small for your purposes will probably slow you down in getting to your destination or capsize in rough weather. What you need, therefore, is to build a business aligned with your purpose that will take you to your vision as efficiently as possible. Taking care of this also means the whole process of actualizing your vision will be fulfilling and rewarding, for all the people involved: you, your family, your team, and your clients (as well as the community at large, if that forms part of your ambition).

In Part II, we will focus on the key elements of a strong business foundation. These form part of the SCALE-UP system – namely the "C.A.L.E." components. Each will be described in detail in a separate chapter; getting an overview of how they fit together will be useful, though:

- Core Purpose: The "why" of your company. What impact do you want to create through your business? How do you plan to improve your clients' lives?

- Core Values and Guiding Principles: What ideas are fundamental guiding tools for business decisions and building your culture and tribe?

- Core Focus: What is your specialization? How does this focus infuse the business and its people with energy, productiveness, and ambition?

Together, these three elements form the core competencies of your business.

Core Strengths:

Ambitious Vision: This element focuses and directs your business at a destination that your team can work toward in unison. Just like a personal success vision, a good business vision is inspiring, holistic, and attainable. One important distinction here is that, where your business is concerned, we're talking about a collective vision shared with your team, not an individual dream.

Leadership: Leadership starts with oneself (self-leadership). What kind of leadership mindset will guide your vision? How will this inspire your team, your clients, and other stakeholders on your collective journey to success? Effective leaders hire the right people, inspire and motivate them, set clear goals and expectations, and provide guidance and direction. All of this starts with embracing the right mindset.

Elite Team: A business is only as strong as the people who drive it forward. By finding good fits for your culture, complemented by the necessary skills for each job, you can design an elite team that's committed to the company's purpose, values, and the actualization of your vision.

My objective is for the following chapters to equip you with all the elements needed to create your thriving and fulfilling company, whatever your definition of this may be. By the end of Part II, you will be clear about your business's purpose. You and your team will be thrilled and excited about the destination you are journeying toward. You already have a mental picture of the smiling, sweaty group picture on the summit of a mountain in mind: a proud and fulfilled team. Even more importantly, you know that the journey itself will be a source of joy. You appreciate that, by the end, every one of you will have stretched, grown, and experienced greatness in your own individual way while serving your chosen community (each other, your clients, and the world).

Let's build to thrive!

CHAPTER 5

CORE STRENGTHS – YOUR VALUE PROPOSITIONS TO YOUR CLIENTS, YOUR EMPLOYEES, AND THE WORLD

"Instant success is never possible. Competence results only from sustained, consistent, self-disciplined effort over an extended period of time"

– Bud Wilkinson, football player and coach.

What are the core strengths that enable success? A generic response will not create a roadmap to success; everybody needs to find answers that are unique to them. At the same time, these core strengths need to apply to an entire business and its workforce. Defining a company's core strengths starts with its leader, but also involves every single employee.

What sets you apart and gives you an edge over your competition? I've found that this is easier to identify by using the three 3 Cs: Core Purpose, Core Values and Core Focus.

- **Core Purpose** – The impact your organization makes on the world around you. This answers the question "Why?" of your business.

- **Core Values** – A set of principles which governs how you conduct your business. This shapes your tribe and culture, and supports your decision-making.

- **Core Focus** – The specialization of your organization, which has a direct effect on its productivity and focus.

Together, these core strengths define your corporate identity, guide your behaviours, and ultimately provide you with the stability and strength you need to overcome whatever challenges you may find in your path. They facilitate your productivity, and ultimately your fulfilling and thriving business.

Let's use the hiking metaphor again: imagine a scenario where one team is on an ambitious hike to a summit that they have never climbed before. They have a clear idea about why reaching the top is important and are quite motivated, not only for themselves but for their companions (because they care about their team, deeply). They are well prepared to make collective decisions if unexpected obstacles show up along the way and also know in their hearts that the summit they chose is achievable. They are confident in their team's strength and purpose.

Now imagine a different team on an equally ambitious hike. The members of this team have no clear idea about why they are trying to scale this mountain in the first place. A few of them have already begun grumbling; soon enough, as blisters develop and the path to the top becomes less clear, others begin expressing their resentment toward each other. They start experiencing friction and forming cliques, paralyzing their decision-making when obstacles arise. Eventually, a few members decide to leave: they are not feeling fulfilled and realize that their core values will be better served elsewhere.

This slows down the journey for those who remain: they now need to recruit new teammates to help carry the load and catch up with the scheduled plan. It's not clear which people will be a good fit, though: instead of a cohesive unit, this so-called "team" is a collection of individuals with widely differing ideas on how to get things done. The team's morale is inevitably low. They have a nagging feeling that the summit is beyond their reach and a pointless effort in any case. Their performance is, at best, lacklustre. They don't know what they are capable of, either individually or when they all pull together.

Needless to say, we are aiming to be like the first team. Let's dive deeper into each core strength.

Your Action:

Take a Good Look at Core Strengths that Bind a Team to a Common Purpose – Examine what works to bring a business together.

Outlining your core strengths is essential to provide direction to your leadership and build a motivated, unified team that's excited about their shared goals. We'll examine how to define and implement your core purpose, core values, and core focus in the next few chapters. For now, though, spend a few minutes on the following brainstorming exercise:

1. Think back to all the companies and organizations you've been involved with. Which had unfocused, unmotivated employees working at cross-purposes? Which, by contrast, had a dedicated workforce who knew exactly what they were about? Which had leaders everyone admired and gladly followed?

2. What core strengths can you identify in those organizations that run smoothly? How have you seen successful managers and entrepreneurs embody these?

CHAPTER 6

CORE PURPOSE – YOUR GIFT TO THE WORLD: YOUR BUSINESS'S "WHY", YOUR CAUSE, THE COMMON THREAD THAT ATTRACTS STAKEHOLDERS TO YOUR BUSINESS

"The purpose of life is to discover your gift. The work of life is to develop it. The meaning of life is to give your gift away."

– David Viscott, American psychiatrist,
author, businessman, and media personality.

One of the two hiking teams we met in the previous chapter is almost certainly going to make it; the other is extremely likely to fail. The only fundamental difference between the two, which may be comprised of equally talented individuals, is knowing why they are going on this hike in the first place. Once you have a clear purpose established for everyone involved, you will almost automatically attract a team that cherishes and embraces your cause because it also harmonizes with who they are.

This begins with you, the leader. What is your life purpose? How does your business purpose support it? Remember: almost everything of importance you do should be based on your personal vision. When you start from the absolute basics, as it were, you'll be surprised at how much more purposeful your life becomes and how things tend to come together even without active effort on your part.

My own life purpose is to help people live fulfilling lives. How does my business purpose support it? My business is to help the leaders of small enterprises live fulfilling lives through making their companies thrive. See how my intentions, my goals, and my actions align perfectly? They only rarely come into conflict. When faced with a challenge or difficult decision, I almost always know what to do right away.

Let's have a look at your own life goals, and try to condense these into a core purpose. What is the positive impact you want to create with your organization? The core purpose comes down to impact. It's the reason for the existence of your business.

Core purpose is the main positive impact you create for your clients and other stakeholders. It goes beyond the financial aspects of your company and defines the meaning behind your business activities.

The core purpose becomes a rallying cry and attracts your tribe, be it your employees, clients, suppliers, and even random people interacting with you on the internet. It dictates how you work with them. As an aside, companies with a clear core purpose tend to be those recognized for excellent customer service.

Just like your personal life purpose, your business purpose will be your North Star which guides your general direction. You may feel like this is still too abstract and academic a concept for an entrepreneur determined to make it in the real world. However, I've seen plenty of companies without a business purpose fail, and those with one succeed against the odds. Here are some examples of the core purposes of brands that defied all initial expectations:

- **Google:** "To organize the world's information and make it universally accessible and useful."

- **Tesla:** "To accelerate the world's transition to sustainable energy."

- **Airbnb:** "To help create a world where you can belong anywhere and where people can live in a place, instead of just travelling to it."

- **Patagonia:** "Build the best product, cause no unnecessary harm, use business to inspire and implement solutions to the environmental crisis."

All of these core purposes are inherently meaningful and inspiring to the company owners and equally so to their teams. They become a rallying point for like-minded clients and employees, because they can easily tell what the business stands for. All of these examples give the feeling of being part of something bigger than oneself, which is a very human yearning, located deep within each of us. To this end, note that the core purposes of all of the companies above are framed in largely positive terms. If BP defined its core purpose as "Not spilling 3 million barrels of oil into the Gulf of Mexico – again", how well do you think that would motivate its stakeholders?

Your core purpose should be more than just a corporate buzzword. If you treat it as a checkbox you are expected to tick to keep up with current trends, you won't get any benefit from it. When embraced fully, however, the business purpose will be visible in all of your operations. Each employee, no matter their position in the organization, will know their role and can develop a passion for the direction the organization is heading. They feel more fulfilled and engaged with their work. On paper, this means lower turnover rates, but the benefits of having a clear core purpose for your company manifest in numerous other ways.

For example, several of my clients run overseas education consulting businesses. Without a core purpose, their teams are simply selling education programs day in, and day out. Their day-to-day tasks can become mundane for both the owners and their employees. Just servicing one client after another with various wants and needs gets old quickly. How does having a core purpose turn this around?

When an education consulting business recognizes its core purpose, employees aren't just selling education programs. They're playing a role in helping their clients build successful careers, potentially improving the lives of dozens or hundreds of people through their recommendations. They live fulfilling lives as a result. Who doesn't like coming home knowing that they made a positive impact on someone's life that day? Helping someone find a good education provides the first step on their journey towards their personal goals. Once what they do was reframed with a meaningful purpose, going to work became an event to look forward to.

Meeting with clients is now a different experience for her consultants, while the clients feel heard and empowered. Employees feel that they're part of something bigger. They are more fulfilled in their work, and their decision-making is informed by the fact that they are helping to create their clients' futures. They are putting the dreams and aspirations of each potential student at the forefront of their minds – and are all the more effective due to this fact. This is how core purpose changes things. Today, there is a clear motivation for each of them to do their best. Every one of their workdays is more meaningful.

Not every business begins with a core purpose in mind. In my experience, it's rare that my clients had a clearly defined core purpose when they first started working with me, which may have delayed their creation of a viable company culture. However, if you currently do not have a core purpose, don't worry. You are not alone.

Serve to Thrive

I strongly believe that a business built to serve clients is destined to thrive. That has been my cumulative experience during the past three decades of working with hundreds of businesses and their leaders. It's also a concept that can be found front and centre in numerous management manuals. Expanding on this idea in a way that encourages your employees simply increases the potential upside.

We have all, from time to time, experienced great service in our interactions with various organizations, from healthcare providers to retail stores. We can sense when they truly care about us even more than their own short-term profit (Long-term profitability, of course, is largely built on satisfied customers.)

Last year, Håkan and I switched to a different dentist. The experience with the new one has been exactly what I've been describing – everyone who works there truly cares about their patients, from the receptionist to the hygienist to the dentist. It's not that this office somehow managed to hire more dedicated people. It's clearly stemming from a collective understanding of what their core purpose is: "We believe in patient-centred care".

Considering the bad rep that some dentists have, for instance by recommending dental work that is not necessary but will make them more money, this dentist is different. They have placed our health, not their profit, at the core of their business. Loyalty provides their long-term gain.

We've not been recommended one procedure we didn't need, but instead were told about effective preventative care. Since this year has been an interesting one for me due to other health challenges, the whole office was aware of my troubles and cared about my journey at all levels.

Having been a business leader and coach for as long as I have, it's a habit of mine to assess small businesses and their culture whenever I interact with them. This dental clinic, for example, has done quite a few things right. All of it, though, started with defining their core purpose. They have their customers' well-being at the heart of their business. I know this because that's been Håkan's and my experience consistently at all levels. This was not a box-ticking exercise for them: they actively and consistently pursue and live their core purpose.

Then, we have is the opposite kind of customer experience. There is a hardware store near us, a franchise operation. This specific location is well-sited in the neighbourhood. It should benefit from its strategic positioning; in addition, their products are well-priced. It could have really brought in customers, again and again, if they cared about service.

Yet it has only a little over 1 out of 5-star rating on Google, due entirely to how it treats its external stakeholders and the employees within the company. Because it is so conveniently located for us when we want to combine our shopping, we tried the store several times, on each occasion hoping that we had simply had a bad experience that wouldn't be repeated again. After several consistently uninspired visits, though, we finally decided that we needed to vote with our money and not patronize this store ever again. Note that most dissatisfied customers don't complain but simply leave. This is just one way failing to establish your core purpose invisibly hurts your business – while emphasizing it works for you silently but constantly.

It's always sad to see a company lose its way completely because its leaders never really thought about the impact they want to have on the world. Usually, several different things indicate to me that it lacks a core purpose. If such a business does have one, it is simply: "Make money for the owners." This means there's nothing driving the employees to deliver exceptional service to customers except their paychecks.

As you can see from these examples (and probably several more drawn from your own life), having a business purpose is indeed important. When your business's core purpose involves serving the community as a whole, each of your employees will be that much more motivated to go above and beyond. By contrast, predatory or exploitative businesses tend not to last long or attract the best kind of employees and stakeholders.

Customers, suppliers, and other stakeholders like to see that your business cares about them. Many will want to see that the brand cares about the wider world as well, because they do. So how do you create a culture like our dentist's office rather than the hardware store? One that delights customers, suppliers, contractors, and in fact the employees themselves, instead of repelling them?

The Importance of Engaging Your Team in the Core Purpose Building

Solopreneurs are in a pretty special position regarding their companies: many of these enterprises are essentially marketing tools for their own time and expertise. While there may be some people who help them out with specific tasks, they are basically one-woman (or one-man) shows. This means that their personal visions and the core purpose for their businesses overlap considerably.

Your situation may be very different, with dozens to hundreds of employees who rely on you. The procedure for defining a core purpose remains much the same as for a company operated by a single person, with one major difference: the importance of getting input from your entire workforce. It is possible to try to impose a business's core purpose from the top down, but you're unlikely to see anything like the best possible results from this approach.

If it's not just yourself who will determine your business's success, engage your whole team in drafting your core purpose. As a leader, you have to recognize that your own aspirations aren't going to drive the organization forward. A company becomes an ecosystem that breathes, evolves, and changes. Your influence will be crucial, but each person in your organization can impact how your core business purpose is pursued. It's prudent for you to get your team's buy-in, and this is a lot easier when you give your employees a chance to shape and give feedback on your core purpose. You will most likely be pleasantly surprised by the insights that your team provides.

Most small business owners have become used to making decisions on their own. You probably started your operations with just yourself or perhaps a few other people, and haven't really involved others in the process of setting the overall course. However, allowing other people to have strategic input is a skill you will need to master, especially once you're scaling up your business and employing a bigger team.

Creating a mindset that this is OUR company (versus MY company) is crucial to a succesful scale-up. Your daily operations, as well as working towards a shared core purpose, are now a team sport, not an individual event. Instead of you being the star player, you will be shifting toward a role similar to a coach leading an elite team. This distinction will serve you well as your business grows and it becomes increasingly difficult to juggle everything by yourself.

Reflect on the Past Evolution of Your Core Purpose

The first step to creating a core purpose is to think about the past. Ask yourself: "What positive impact did I intend to have through my business when I started it?" We want to nail down our original intention when we created our business. For example, you may have started a photography business with the goal of: "Helping families capture the most precious moments of their children." You may have started an immigration consulting business to "Help Latin Americans build their dream life in Canada."

It's fine if you've drifted somewhat from your original goals. The examples above are more specific than the typical core purpose that defines the impact you want your business to have. Note, too, how these definitions help us identify important stakeholders and areas of specialization, both of which will be handy later on.

Most businesses, whether recent startups or established companies, have to make course corrections from time to time. Wedding photography may have proven to be more lucrative than you thought at first, and the pictures you take now are equally special to your clients. Perhaps you now advise your client base not just on visa issues, but help them search for accommodation and jobs. In either case, though your business's focus has evolved, you are still travelling in roughly the same direction and following the same North Star. What we need to do now is balance your current reality with your original intent.

To this purpose, assess what you do in your current business operations. Does your original core purpose still apply or has the motive behind your activities changed? To use the immigration consulting example, your operations may have expanded; now, you're helping Latin Americans make a fresh start in Canada, the U.K., and Australia. Conversely, you may have narrowed your focus to serve only highly skilled professionals. Whether your core purpose is broader or more narrowly directed, it is high time to reflect on these changes. Most business's core purposes will evolve during the lifetime of the company, even if ever so slightly. With you still at the helm, however, the essence of what you hope to accomplish won't change.

The next step is to look ahead into the future while still allowing your business's legacy to guide you. What impact do you aspire to make, going forward? What legacy do you want your business to have built once you've reached your goals? Think beyond financial targets and consider the broader impact your organization can have on society as a whole, the environment, or specific communities. How can your business contribute to a better world? Define the positive change or difference you aim to create through your offering.

Now, while you are doing this, remember that there's nothing wrong with wanting to make money. I am certainly not encouraging you to go broke, in which case you won't be able to help anybody. Let's take a moment to look at the mechanics behind starting a profitable business, though. If you have an idea of how to genuinely serve others, it's almost certainly possible to monetize it in some way. Approaching the same project from the opposite direction – beginning with nothing but a desire to be rich – doesn't help you determine either a business concept or its core purpose. You may end up peddling a product or service nobody is truly interested in. You'll have constructed a boat that may look pretty cool but is entirely unsuited to travel your chosen waters.

Draft Your Core Purpose

Once you have brainstormed all three aspects – your original motivation, current business realities, and your future aspirations – ask yourself: "What core purpose would balance all three in my business decisions while also inspiring my current and future clients and other stakeholders to make a better world? The world can be your immediate environment – your employees, investors, clients, and their families. Or it can be a much bigger community.

It seems to be a characteristic of effective core purpose statements that they're simple to read and share, but hard to create. Take your time and go through several iterations if you need to. Lean on your employees and stakeholders. They'll be happy to help and may have valuable perspectives or insights on elements you tend to overlook.

Write down your core purpose. If you feel uncertain about it or as if it's not complete, place it somewhere you'll see it for the next few days and try to think of refinements. The next step, once you think you've arrived at a winning core purpose, is to validate and develop it further. I've found the "multiple wins test" to be very useful for this purpose. This is like a touchstone for a purpose you'd be glad to pursue.

The basis of this exercise is to see if various different stakeholders will benefit from you pursuing this goal, and that none will be harmed. A strong core purpose should create a:

- Win for clients – How does it contribute to making their lives better?

- Win for your team – How does it allow them to grow and thrive?

- Win for your business – How does it benefit your business, financially, in terms of reputation, or in other ways?

- Win for the world – How does it contribute to making the world a better place?

- Win for yourself – How does it bring you closer to living your ideal life?

If we look back to Patagonia's core purpose ("Build the best product, cause no unnecessary harm, use business to inspire and implement solutions to the environmental crisis."), we can see how it generates wins for everybody. With this core purpose, the company sowed the seeds of a company that benefits all its stakeholders instead of being predatory in some sense.

Another example of how the "multiple wins test" can help you to analyze and refine your core purpose comes from my client, Rachel Yoon's Photography (RYP). Her business core purpose states: "Be a vehicle to create and preserve happy memories for families through quality photography." Now, let's see how this holds up in practice:

- The clients' win – Creating happy memories during the photography sessions and receiving high-quality images of those precious moments so they can re-live them forever.

- The team's win – Fulfilling and enjoyable work that provides a wonderful experience to the families they serve.

- The business win – Happy customers mean repeat business and referrals, which creates a sustainable and profitable business. Fulfilled employees stay longer and provide high-quality and consistent service to their clients.

- The owner's win – Happy stakeholders mean a happy business owner. Rachel is leading a fulfilling life now and her future holistic life vision is being achieved through work she loves.

By working with happy clients and satisfied employees, within the framework of a stable and well-known business, Rachel is getting that much closer to achieving her personal core purpose. Also note how each of these "wins" underlies one another. If subjecting your core business purpose to the "multiple wins test" shows that it tramples on the needs of employees, clients, or yourself, you need to take another crack at defining it.

Define Your Core Purpose so that It Is Clear, Concise, and Concrete and Embed It in All Your Operations

Did your business core purpose pass "the multiple wins" test? If not, it is time to wordsmith your core purpose until it is something you are excited to share with everyone. Keep your definition clear, concise, and concrete (the 3 Cs I refer to often). Clear and concise to make it easier to know by heart and easy to internalize, and concrete so that no misunderstandings can arise. If we don't precisely know what it is we do, it's hard to be guided by a core purpose.

Once you have defined your core purpose, communicate it to all employees through whatever means works best for your organization. Your core purpose is not useful if nobody knows what it is. Don't let it gather dust in a desk drawer. Instead, make sure to embed it in all of your business operations. Refer to it often in meetings, emails, and other contact points. If your employees are calibrating their ideas to coincide with your core purpose and actively suggest new ways you can further your purpose, then it's working effectively for you.

The first place to start may be a special staff meeting everyone is expected to attend. Share and explain your core purpose and discuss how you can all get involved in actualizing this goal. Prompt your team to think about what it will look like in practice; help them to integrate it into their lives. Using this joint forum brings everyone together under one core purpose, ties them together as a unified crew, and builds team spirit. Again, the feeling of being part of something bigger than yourself is universally inspiring and motivating. This is often the single factor that differentiates organizational cultures that result in excellence from mediocre ones.

You may include this exercise as part of each quarterly staff meeting and repeat it periodically in other forums. Make sure the agenda always includes the question: "How are we living our core purpose?" Reinforce purpose-supporting behaviours by rewarding team members appropriately. This may take the form of compliments delivered individually or in public during business meetings. Don't be afraid of pointing out if someone's actions run contrary to your business's core purpose.

One thing I've noticed is how, when my clients get their teams involved in the process of defining their company's core purpose, they become even more inspired by the ideas their colleagues suggested. The shared excitement is contagious. Crafting a clear, concise, and concrete core purpose and sharing it in the right way means all those around you will be newly invigorated and eager to implement the resulting ideas.

Your Action:

Define Your Core Purpose – Establish what will be the motivator of your people.

1. Draft your business's core purpose by balancing your original intentions that led you to founding your business, current reality, and future aspirations. If you have employees, engage them.

2. Make sure that this core purpose ensures wins for all engaged: your team, your clients, and whoever else may be involved.

3. Define your core purpose and ensure that it is clear, concise and concrete. These are essential requirements for sharing it.

4. Communicate your core purpose to all stakeholders. Encourage feedback, and make sure it's at the forefront of everyone's minds.

5. Create a plan to make your core purpose come alive in your organization. Include it as an agenda item in your staff meeting, and make sure your people development process is aligned with this goal.

CHAPTER 7

CORE VALUES & GUIDING PRINCIPLES – THE CULTURE AND GLUE OF YOUR TRIBE AND A GUIDE ON HOW TO BUILD A UNIFIED CREW

"Your personal core values define who you are, and a company's core values ultimately define the company's character and brand. For individuals, character is destiny. For organizations, culture is destiny."

– Tony Hsieh, former CEO of Zappos

The first time I came to know about Tony Hsieh was while I was preparing a workshop for our executive leadership team as their chief marketing officer. I ran across a description of the footwear company Zappos's core values first and was quite impressed by them. This led me to start reading more about the company's culture. After a while, I just had to buy shoes from them myself to assess this culture from a customer's perspective. In short, the customer service people I spoke to and all the experiences I've had with Zappos consistently demonstrated their core values. I became a fan and, although I no longer buy shoes (I've got plenty, considering my sustainable lifestyle), those early interactions with the company truly impressed me.

When I worked as chief marketing officer, I used to tell my team that every single member, including myself, could be replaced. As with a car engine or a desktop computer, the whole is greater than the sum of its parts and can keep on functioning perfectly even if one component is switched out with another.

The one thing that could not be replaced is the team as a collective entity. Our department had an excellent reputation within the industry, enjoyed working with each other, respected their colleagues, and felt like a big family. Each member was willing to vigorously (yet respectfully) defend their standpoints because there was a high level of trust. There weren't many "yes-men" and both management and workers supported their collective decisions and worked in unison. Significantly, this was despite the fact that we had individual team members from more than fifteen different cultural backgrounds who spoke multiple languages between them.

Working together felt a lot like being a member of a family, and "family" is the key word here. We had all found our tribe and were proud of being part of this team. There is one year I remember especially vividly. We were competing for an industry award; our client network would vote for their most effective partners. The winner would be determined by who delivered the best service and operational experiences, as well as quality training, to those who bought from them.

We were up against some serious industry heavyweights and needed all our different country representatives to garner support from their clients. Meanwhile, the marketing team needed to create communication and promotion strategies in conjunction with the sales team. These collaborative efforts as well as their individual ones were a beautiful thing to watch. It wasn't hard to see that there was a strong commitment, not only to each person's own success, but also to that of the team as a whole. We had some spirited debates around how and when to launch the campaigns but, once a decision was made, there was no question about everyone's focus and commitment to this collective goal. Just in case you were wondering, we did win! The elation we felt was out of this world.

Earlier, I described a group picture of a smiling, sweaty team taken on a summit they'd just scaled. This is a good metaphor for those moments of peak achievement that can be reached by a team that has embraced its core strengths (core purpose, core values, and core focus). There's a good chance that you'll relate to this analogy if you have been part of a strong team effort and culture. How about your colleagues at work? Is there a strong bond between all of you? Is it anything like working with family?

Everything else being equal, a strong culture leads to a thriving business. Not paying attention to this prerequisite for a company's success is like setting sail in a boat without a compass: there's a small chance that navigating at random will bring you to your destination, but that's not the way to bet.

The Advantages Core Values and Company Culture Offer

So, in specific terms, how does having a strong culture benefit a company? As we've already mentioned, their customer satisfaction ratings tend to soar. Not only will employees cooperate more smoothly with one another, they will take pride in their work and their company's reputation. There's just no comparison between this state of affairs and a business in which staff are more concerned with watching the clock, ticking boxes, and doing only enough to keep their jobs.

Another effect of emphasizing culture is that having this strong team identity in place makes it much simpler to hire new employees. This is because you'll consistently be hiring with your culture, and how candidates will slot into it, in mind. It's easy to spot who doesn't belong to your tribe. Considering that its team is the strongest asset a business can have in its SCALE-UP, the importance of choosing the right people for your elite team cannot be overemphasized. When something does go wrong with the hiring process, you will notice the new, "bad fit" employee sticking out like a sore thumb. They too will realize they don't belong to the tribe.

A further advantage of a well-established culture is that it eventually becomes a tool for employee empowerment. When the company's values and established practices make some decision obvious, there's no reason to bother a superior with it. In this regard, hiring the right people is particularly important for small business owners: a strong culture means that your business continues to thrive even when you take a step back from the day-to-day operations. You alone will no longer need to be the "glue" that holds everything together. Many entrepreneurs are not yet ready to contemplate a more strategic role or even retirement, but revisiting your personal vision of an ideal life may show that starting to plan and prepare for this is prudent. In any case, a team whose leader who can be replaced with another capable individual is stronger than any group that relies on constant direction from a single manager.

More About Culture and Hiring Practices

In his book *Good to Great*, Jim Collins provides a quote that exemplifies the way in which I encourage my clients to think about hiring and retaining staff.

"First, get the right people on the bus, the wrong people off the bus, and the right people in the right seats."

It isn't hard to understand the importance of hiring and retaining individuals who align with the organization's core values (right people) and have the necessary skills and capabilities (right seats) to drive its success.

My clients Mark and Paula were recently looking for a new head of marketing, which is a key role in their organization. It was crucial for them to get this right; remembering their core values while reviewing applicants helped a great deal. Finding a candidate who had the right skills and experience for the role was important, certainly. However, their outlook also had to match the core values of the business. Any member of the team needs to dovetail with the tribe but, in the case of a head of marketing, it is even more critical to choose a good fit. After all, this person will be responsible for creating marketing communications exhibiting the corporate culture to new clients and employees.

Instead of being discouraged by this criterion, the candidate quickly embraced this company's focus on its core values. She was looking for long-term employment in which she could grow professionally and contribute to building a business, all while being part of a strong team. Once she learned about the company's core values, she was reassured that this would be a good position for someone with her personality and mindset. She could therefore make an informed decision instead of guessing at what the company's culture was like. Core values are not only valuable tools for a business hoping to build an elite team; they also enable employees to find their tribe and a fulfilling workplace more easily – further reducing the incidence of hiring decisions that have to be undone later.

Using Core Values and Culture in Practice

Core values aren't just valuable in the recruitment process. Applied correctly, they can improve all aspects of your business, benefiting multiple stakeholders.

Think back to some particularly difficult managerial decisions you had to make in the past. What bothered you about them and made them so hard? Sometimes, you simply have to select a course of action without knowing its likely outcome or accept the lesser of two evils. Decisions involving staff are often the most important ones, hence our heavy focus on them in this chapter. Notwithstanding, we make choices of various kinds all day long, be they selecting a vendor, client, expansion direction, or core focus.

Business core values are fundamental beliefs and principles that guide and shape our business identity, behaviours, and decision-making. They reflect what is important, meaningful, and non-negotiable to our organization. When selected and phrased with care, they tend to transcend specific situations or contexts and remain consistent over time.

Business core values provide a strong foundation upon which to build your organizational culture. They shape attitudes, actions, and relationships both within and outside of the organization.

The two groups who gain most from a business having clear core values are your employees and clients:

- Your employees appreciate core values because they define the expected behaviours, attitudes, and norms within the organization. The right core values foster a positive and supportive work environment, encourage collaboration, and create a sense of belonging and fulfillment. Employees who share these core values will feel like they have found a workplace where they not only fit in but can thrive. They spend their days doing work that is meaningful to them, leading to higher productivity and better employee retention.

- Your clients benefit from core values through getting a consistent experience in all their dealings with your company. Instead of getting wildly different results each time based on who they speak to or which department they interact with, they can expect to receive dependable service aligned with the business core values. Whether in routine or exceptional situations, the company's responses are dictated by the same principles.

All of this translates to huge benefits for your business. Employees with a strong sense of belonging to their team, accompanied by an affinity for your values and guiding principles, serve your clients to a high standard. Their persistent embodiment of your business core values differentiates you from your competitors. Should your clients perceive that your business follows similar values to theirs (as opposed to simply saying you do), you'll attract additional like-minded clients. Existing ones are also more likely to remain loyal to your company, just like myself with Zappos and the numerous companies my former marketing and sales team serve.

Uncovering the Core Values of Your Business

The process of defining your business's core values has a lot in common with discovering your business's core purpose, as we did in the previous chapter. You could, potentially, just scribble them down on a piece of paper and declare the job finished. However, following a structured series of steps – not entirely dissimilar from the one for discovering your personal core values we covered in Chapter 2 – makes the process much easier and will leave you feeling much more confident in the results.

Mine Your Core Values

An excellent starting point is to examine the roots and later evolution of your company before peering into the future.

Ask yourself the following questions to identify your past intentions:

- How did I want to conduct my business when I first started my company?

- What values did I expect to guide me in my business dealings, interactions, and decisions?

Review Your Current Values

Once you have a list of the core values you started out with, consider your current reality. What values still hold true; which are less applicable? For various reasons, a few may have become less relevant over time, been superseded by more important values, or fallen by the wayside completely.

A common scenario is that you started as a solopreneur but now employ a team, requiring a different outlook. Remember, once you hire your first employee, the business is no longer just "yours", whatever its articles of incorporation say. In an intangible yet important sense, it belongs to the collective. If you have a team, I recommend you engage them in the brainstorming process and actively solicit their insights.

Add Your Aspirational Values

Now that you have a list of values drawn from the past and expanded, with the help of your current team, to reflect the present, think about what kind of company you'd like to be. Imagine your future best "business self", one which personifies your business purpose. We haven't established our business vision yet, which we will do in short order. In the meantime, you will still have some ideas as to what success may involve. What values do you need to add to become your best self? How do you want your stakeholders to describe your organization? What characteristics does your ideal tribe possess?

For example, your future success may involve expanding into multiple branches from the current one-store operation. This would increase the importance of values related to accountability, as you would not all be working in one location anymore. How about communication? If accountability and communication are not part of your current core values, they should probably find their way onto the list.

Define Your Core Values

The next step is to integrate the listed values that are currently valid and the new ones that will help you achieve future success. The idea is to create a shortlist containing no more than five values (just like we did when identifying our personal values). Including more just dilutes the impact of the most important ones.

It may take a significant amount of time to arrive at your final five entries. This is an important process, so you may want to schedule two or three sessions to complete it to your satisfaction. Arranging these on different days helps you generate fresh insights, while taking some time in between to process your thoughts may also lead to more precise and definite results.

Once you've worked through this process, you'll have your core business values. These will prove invaluable in guiding your future business decisions and inspiring your team on the journey to deliver your vision. Now that you have this incredibly helpful tool for efficiently choosing between various alternatives, I sincerely hope you will use it. Yes, I have indeed seen leaders who are at first very excited about their core values, then somehow completely forget to apply them.

Help Realize Your Values by Setting Guiding Principles

Just like in the process of defining your personal values, adding guiding principles to each value makes them more concrete and easier to act on. Instead of being abstract words to get engraved on a plaque and never looked at again, they are expected behaviours for everyone in the company. They may well form the preamble to your employee handbook, prospectus, business plans, and similar documents.

Write down one to three ways in which you want your core values to come alive in your day-to-day operations. Here are some examples to help you create your own.

Integrity:

- Be precise about our deliverables and timeline in the contract
- Deliver what we promise – 100% of the time

Quality of Work:

- Be accurate in our documentation
- Predict operational challenges and proactively address them

Broadcast Your Core Values

Your core values and guiding principles are no good to anyone if they are hidden away in a notebook or desk drawer. As far as realizing your vision is concerned, this is just as effective as shouting at a referee through the TV screen.

Consistent and effective communication of your business core values fosters a shared understanding and commitment to these values throughout your company. This, in turn, starts to forge that crucial company culture. Here are some examples of ways to communicate your core values:

- Display visual representations of the core values throughout the workplace and on your website.

- Reinforce the core values in internal communications via success stories in newsletters, team meetings, and on the intranet and internet.

- Integrate your business values into HR processes so that they are central to hiring, onboarding, training, performance reviews, and leadership development decisions.

- Share your core values externally through marketing materials and website content.

- Demonstrate core values through corporate social responsibility initiatives.

When disseminating and reinforcing your core values to an internal audience, remember to explain the significance of the values, the expected behaviours attached to them, and how they guide your organization's culture and operations. You want your leaders and employees alike to understand and appreciate these values, and their guiding principles, before asking them to adhere to them.

As we discussed previously, I cannot emphasize enough how important it is to involve your entire team in the value-definition process, as their buy-in will be so much greater. You can then expect a much deeper commitment from them once the final values have been decided on. This is another topic you may want to add to the agenda of a meeting to which all staff are invited. Workshop it the way you did for your core purpose.

Build and Maintain an Admirable Tribe Using Your Core Values

Workplace culture is going to be one of the first things your new employees and potential clients notice about your company. Without a strong culture, based not only on productivity but also fulfillment, it becomes much harder to succeed in almost any industry.

Culture is about creating an environment conducive to achieving your business vision while also allowing your tribe to thrive. You are hiking to a lofty summit together. Your values provide a compass to guide you in decision-making as well as providing a centre for your culture to develop around. Once these elements are in place, your mutual journey will be immeasurably more joyful and fulfilling. You will hike an ever-ascending path with people you trust and respect. Your smiling, sweaty group picture will one day reflect your pride in your own achievement, but even more so in everyone's shared sense of accomplishment.

Your tribe should be an elite team that is aligned with the core values of the company. This happens when business values and vision resonate with employees' personal ones. When building your tribe, therefore, it's crucial to establish each person's cultural fit as well as hiring for ability and experience. If you recall the Jim Collins quote, we're aiming to get the right people on the bus (culture) and in the right seats (skills).

The uncomfortable truth is that, sometimes, you also need to get the wrong people off the bus. Some of your current team members may not belong in the tribe you are building. There are no "bad" core values, yet a bad fit between different sets of core values is entirely possible. If someone does not jibe with your business values, it simply means that your organization is not an environment where they will thrive. In this case, it means they're almost certainly bound to become an obstacle to your vision and will be happier elsewhere.

Consider plants: some thrive in harsh sunlight, and others enjoy dark shade. Either may produce beautiful, fragrant flowers, but you simply can't put both kinds of plants in the same environment and expect all of them to flourish.

If one of your business core values is "customer satisfaction" and you've hired a stickler for the rules whose highest personal value is "order" or "fairness", that could spell trouble if that employee isn't sufficiently adaptable. Or, if your business values growth and expansion but you've hired a change-averse employee who prioritizes stability and security, you may need to consider Jim Collins's bus analogy again. Transplant the shade-loving plants into a shadowy garden if they aren't doing well in a sunny backyard. Even better, ensure that your sun-friendly plants are raised in an open, sunny garden in the first place. A new hire or existing employee who turns out to be a "bad fit" drains time, effort, productivity, and serenity for everyone involved.

The best way to ensure that you're hiring and retaining the right kinds of people is to embed your core values into your hiring, training, and rewarding process. (You'll find more on this later in Chapter 11, on elite teams.)

Your Action:

Build an Admirable Tribe and Guard It Fiercely – Allow your business core values to guide your hiring decisions and drive your company culture.

A company's culture largely determines its reputation and level of success in its industry. You can't buy, dictate, borrow, or create culture from nothing, though. It has to be built, using your business core values and supporting guiding principles as a foundation.

1. Define your business core values considering your original intention, current reality, and future aspirations.

2. Shortlist them to no more than five items.

3. Establish 1 to 3 guiding principles for each core value.

4. Communicate them company-wide as well as externally.

5. Integrate values into policies on hiring, training, and rewarding your people.

6. Reinforce values in your general meetings just the way you did with your business core purpose.

CHAPTER 8

CORE FOCUS – YOUR SPECIALIZATION: YOUR REPUTATION AND IRRESISTIBLE OFFER

"What you stay focused on will grow."

– Roy T. Bennett, Author of *Light in the Heart*

A Seoul Story

There is a certain restaurant in Seoul famous for its kimchi-jjigae, a rich, savoury, spicy pork stew. You can find people queuing outside its door every single day, even though they sell nothing but kimchi-jjigae.

They don't serve any variations on their classic recipe, nor anything else except its complimentary side dishes. When customers sit down, they don't get a menu: the staff will simply bring over a bowl of kimchi-jjigae for each person at the table. The bill, too, depends only on the number of diners. There's no difficulty involved in tallying it up, splitting it, or correcting errors (this being South Korea, there isn't even a tip to be calculated). Unless a typhoon is passing by, they never have a shortage of customers. Patrons are willing to wait because this restaurant is well-known as the best at the one thing they do.

In fact, there are many of these single-specialty restaurants in the city. Some examples of their wares are miso stew, braised pork-and-kimchi dishes, cold buckwheat noodles, dumplings, and ribs. What makes this even more remarkable is that Seoul is a city where an enormous number of people crowd into the office districts during the day. There is an equally crazy selection of restaurants, large and small, competing for their business. Yet, every lunchtime, hundreds of people make the trek to a single eatery on a particular city block for kimchi-jjigae.

A one-item menu may seem limiting and not especially appealing to customers. When you think about it, though, operating with such a narrow focus is highly efficient. With a singular purpose, all of their efforts are directed at only one thing and this develops supreme quality, expertise, and if done well, a solid reputation.

Now, compare this approach to that of other restaurants on the same block that sell 50 different dishes, including kimchi-jjigae. If you're a kimchi-jjigae connoisseur or simply feel like having it for lunch, where are you more likely to go? The one specialty restaurant with an established reputation for the dish, or any of those that attempt to cover all possible bases?

Along with their predictably excellent food, you can count on efficiency of service (i.e. no waiting for the food to be prepared, the menu to arrive, or the bill to be delivered). If you only have 30 minutes to one hour for lunch, like most Seoulite office workers, and you wish to also fit some coffee and a walk into your lunchtime routine, you'd be inclined to choose the specialty place. As a customer, you not only benefit from great food but also time, a precious resource.

The Business Benefits of Choosing a Core Focus

How about the business itself – the specialty kimchi-jjigae restaurant? What advantages do they have over competitors who serve multiple dishes?

- Their reputation attracts clients with a particular interest in kimchi stew, thereby increasing sales. (Yes, you may argue that they don't get customers who prefer miso stew, and this is true. More on this topic later.)

- It significantly reduces marketing expenses as market segmentation is much easier and word of mouth does the heavy lifting anyway.

- The single-menu-item concept allows greater operational efficiency, enhancing the customer experience (eg. lower waiting times allowing for more time for other things) and further boosting their reputation.

- Capital expenses, rent, and staff costs are all lower. Simplifying the menu means less equipment, floor space, and fewer cooks are needed.

- Standardization allows for easy scaling. They can easily copy their operational model in a second branch or franchise environment.

- Since they are always operating at maximum capacity, inventory control is simpler. This translates into little to no spoilage, high productivity and profitability.

- They can also plan their labour requirements efficiently. Standardized processes facilitate training of their team. This solidifies their reputation and profitability. There is very little variation in the delivery of the quality of their food and service.

- The lack of divergence and complexity in their operations simplifies decision-making. This allows less involvement by the business owner and affords them more time away from the business.

Far from being restrictive, their narrow focus allows the restaurant to operate at peak efficiency because everything about their operations is predictable. At the same time, their consistent service and quality create an enviable reputation with satisfied customers. This results in sustainable profitability, given that kimchi stew continues to be in demand and the food quality and service efficiency are never less than excellent.

Taking the Specialization Plunge

A business owner is often reluctant to narrow their companies' focus. On the surface, it seems like limiting your client pool or curtailing their options. Logically, wouldn't that also lower your profits?

Looked at in another way, though, specialization is a very efficient method for succeeding as a small player in a competitive industry. It allows businesses to differentiate themselves from others in any given market and devote all of their resources to their special and unique value proposition.

When all other things are equal, customers are indeed likely to choose large generalists over small specialty vendors because they provide more options. Let's say I want to buy some beans – of whatever type – for dinner.

I'll probably go to the supermarket rather than "Legumes 'R' Us", just in case Håkan calls while I'm there and asks me to get asparagus as well.

Speaking generally, customers who don't know exactly what they want aren't good prospects for small, specialized businesses. In addition, small-scale operations can't spend as much on marketing as their larger, jack-of-all-trades counterparts. Considering their limited resources, solopreneurs and small businesses can't afford to try to please all of the people, all of the time. This does not mean they have to give up on being competitive, though.

Now, let's imagine that I'm planning to make a fairly exotic recipe that requires uncommon ingredients, perhaps even kimchi-jjigae. The supermarket probably won't stock them; if they do, their selection and quality will be limited. There almost certainly won't be anyone around who's knowledgeable enough to help me decide on one product over another. In this case, the deciding factor for my shopping destination will probably be the business's reputation. Who has a better reputation for selling excellent tofu, matured kimchi, gochugaru, and other Korean seasonings? In this regard, size doesn't matter. Small businesses enjoy a much better level playing field when they embrace specialization.

Going back to the kimchi stew example, the restaurant specializing in kimchi-jjigae would attract most of the kimchi-jjigae fanatics on any given day. The neighbouring generalist restaurant can still expect to get a few customers from that market segment due to factors like lower prices or some snazzy social media marketing. Still, the gain for the specialist is greater than the opportunity cost of losing other food interest groups. Put another way, it's often better to have a secure hold on 70% of a $10,000-per-day market than hope for 1% of a $100,000-per-day market.

On the opposite side of the coin, what happens when a small business tries to be everything to everyone? Generally speaking, it doesn't have a hope of standing out from the bigger players covering the same field, who have the resources to do several things well. I often see clients who lack this core focus working immensely hard, sacrificing their personal time and even their health to their business's activities only to barely bring home enough profit to support their lifestyles, and sometimes not even that.

Your core focus makes your resource allocation, including your personal schedule, more orderly and predictable. It empowers you to say "no" when something does not fit into your chosen specialization. I call it "empowerment". Your ability to say "no" to whatever would cause you to stray from your specialization empowers you to achieve the balanced and thriving life you hope for. Simply narrowing your business core focus may be your recipe for: "work smart, not hard."

Finding Your Core Focus

Even if you feel your business is already sufficiently focused or niched, I recommend that you work through the following exercises to evaluate your status quo. These questions are designed to help you assess your business operations in an objective manner, and the insights gained can often be surprising.

Like with the other core strengths, defining your core focus is a balancing act between your experience so far and your future aspirations. Your past will inform what made you thrive and what made you falter at times. Using the Pareto Principle, you will be able to identify the most profitable products and services.

The Pareto Principle, also known as the 80/20 rule, states that approximately 80% of an effect arises from 20% of its causes. In business, this generally means that 80% of sales involve 20% of your products and services. It could also be stated that 80% of your profit comes from 20% of your clients.

It will not always be an exact 80/20 split, yet it is often surprisingly close, especially when you combine closely related offerings. For example, my coaching business has two primary service offerings: my signature SCALE-UP program, which guides my clients through the full SCALE-UP framework, and the Executive Business Coaching program, which is made up of part the signature program. Coaching based on the full program represents 50% of my business, teaching the truncated version 30%. So, 80% of my business comes from SCALE-UP coaching.

Your Verticals

Review your past income statements, broken down by product and service types, and look at the volume for each. Combine linked items into verticals. You may have designated product or service verticals already. An accountant, for example, may offer different categories of services: book-keeping, budgeting and financial planning, and auditing. An education consulting business may break down its revenue into language learning, vocational training courses, and college education studies.

Your Gross Sales and Volume

Next, calculate the income each of your verticals earns you. Which ones generate the most sales transactions? Where do most of your earnings come from? These top performers may be two different verticals: one product or service can attract the most customers, even while another brings in more money.

This discrepancy isn't always intuitive, so let's illustrate it. You may have noticed that a few of my clients run education consulting businesses. There are usually a number of products that they sell to students, getting a commission on each sale.

For the sake of example, they might earn 10% of the cost of each ed-ucational course they offer. Let's say they sell four-week language courses (which are $1,000 each) to 100 students and college education programs ($15,000 each) to 20 students. If they looked at the number of sales alone, language programs may look like the best option for them to specialize in. However, when they calculate total sales revenue for each vertical, their college products are a better candidate.

Your Cost of Delivery

It is also crucial to consider the cost of getting each product/service to the customer, i.e. the amount of work and other resources they need to put in to produce and distribute a product or service. For solopreneurs, this most certainly includes their own time; you need to assign a dollar-per-hour value to your own labour.

My SCALE-UP coaching, for example, is usually presented to one or two business owners at a time, whereas my executive coaching generally involves groups of six or more people. I will spend the same amount of time going over the material, whether I interact with one person or a dozen.

My hourly delivery cost is the same, yet I bring in more dollars with group coaching than one-to-one sessions.

With the education consulting example above, think about how long it takes to discuss the options with each student for the two different programs (English versus college studies). The latter requires more time to guide the clients properly; consultants also need additional expertise and may be paid more per hour. However, comparing the revenues generated by a college student and a language learner, over the duration of their respective client journeys, makes it clear that college studies consulting is the more lucrative vertical. As it happens, the marketing cost for attracting clients who want to learn English is also much higher due to low barriers to entry in this sector. Far fewer competitors are able to provide guidance to prospective college students.

It's also worth asking yourself what type of clientele each of your verticals brings you. Does one generate more repeat business and referrals? Is one market segment a better fit for your lifestyle than others? If you must sacrifice some aspect of your fulfilling lifestyle in order to specialize in a particular vertical, that is also a cost to consider.

Incorporate Trends

What tendencies do you see in your own numbers or the industry as a whole? Are your customers' preferences changing in some way? Has your former top-selling product or service underperformed in recent years? Assess whether that is reflected in the industry as a whole; if not, are you losing your competitive edge? Either way, the areas in which you've enjoyed success in the past may not be the right ones to focus on in the future.

You may recall how one of my clients, Mark, chose: "Become a trend-setter in my industry" as his supporting goal. He regularly schedules time in his calendar to actualize it, so new trends rarely catch him by surprise. Most businesses, and smaller ones especially, are always vulnerable to shifts in the market, a changing competitive landscape, or disruptive technological innovations. Taking these into account when setting your business focus can prevent you from going down a fruitless path.

In the example of an education consulting business, the demand for learning English as a second language using in-person classroom programs (outside of the regular school system) may be on the decline. Technological advancement has provided a wider range of options to students of all ages. In the past, relatively wealthy young people may have travelled to English-speaking countries to learn the language. Now, many of these prefer to study at home using various apps, websites, and other platforms.

On the one hand, this trend can spell the end of an education consulting business specializing in language studies. On the other, it actually represents a new opportunity for those who choose the right focus. Students who already have some English may want to pursue higher education or career-orientated training overseas and need to brush up their skills. Improving their fluency and comprehension is now one area in which a company may specialize, divesting the department serving the shrinking ESL sector.

If some such company has already built a team with the necessary knowledge and skills, it could even choose to specialize in a particular field of higher education. The depth of specialization that may be feasible in any given case is determined not only by the potential market size, but also by how well a team and its skills have been curated. Training and recruitment take time; spotting important trends well in advance is crucial to selecting the right business focus.

Be Aspirational

When you review the trends we talked about above, did you see a clear pattern your business could benefit from? During this portion of the exercise, it's best to look primarily at your own financials and sales records; industry experts can't always give you the whole story as it applies to your specific company.

If you don't have the right resources to shift focus immediately, contemplate ways of developing these assets. Perhaps you already have a team member who could pivot into a new role? Maybe your business core values include "adaptability" or "growth mindset". Assuming your team shares these, some may be willing to learn new skills. Alternatively, can you bring in new talent?

I recommend you include analyzing market trends in all quarterly and yearly planning and development sessions. I've already encouraged you to make scheduling these sessions part of your personal productivity system; in your business, involving your team pays great dividends. Plan and prepare your shifts in business focus as soon as trends become clear. The cost of not doing so in a timely manner can be huge, as can the competitive advantage that comes with being a trailblazer.

You will have seen enough examples of what happens when companies aren't able to pivot fast enough and become obsolete instead. How about local bookstores or department stores? Many failed to develop a business core purpose and kept trying to appeal to every single customer out there. Those that adapted in time are still around; others have gone the way of photo labs and phone books.

There may well be a good opportunity in your location and industry that is either currently underserved or delivered ad-hoc or in an amateurish manner. Vinyl records and mechanical watches are both "obsolete", yet they continue to sell – in fact, they're now considered luxury products. Nobody uses VHS tapes or photographic slide projectors anymore, yet this very fact has created an industry around digitizing these formats.

Remember how I urged you to replace to word "challenge" with "opportunity" in your thinking? As the saying goes: "It's an ill wind that blows nobody any good." No matter how threatening a certain trend appears or how unpromising your current prospects are, a shift in focus or increased specialization may be all that's needed to turn things around. Can you provide some kind of competitive offering using your team's unique skill sets and become a frontrunner, even in a relatively small market niche?

RYP, the photography business we became acquainted with earlier, chose newborn baby pictures as its new specialization after realizing that there was a gap in the market in the greater Vancouver area. By specializing in a field that was underserved and underdeveloped, it could compete even with well-established local photography studios. Offering a professional studio setup and high-quality end products made this company stand out from other newborn photographers.

It also helps that the owner is brilliant with babies (so much so that she has earned the nickname "the baby whisperer"), which puts parents at ease. Rachel built her reputation around her core focus relatively quickly despite the fact that she was brand new to the industry. It would've taken her much longer if she tried to be everything to everyone by also doing wedding photography, family portraits, and pet portraits.

Determine Your Core Focus and Specialization

At this point, which product or service strikes you as a winner? Remember, depending on your current scope of operations, you may either change what your business does to something different but not entirely new, or drop other activities in order to commit all your resources to the most lucrative.

Balance factors like revenue per vertical, relative costs, current capabilities, and expected trends to determine which specialization will produce the greatest profit. A good timeline to keep in mind is the next three to five years. You may choose one product/service or a line of business. For example, I could decide on SCALE-UP coaching as the single most productive line, or combine it with Executive Business Coaching – the basic activities and supporting tasks are the same for both.

Choosing a one-item specialization may be a good choice for your business. Håkan's indisputably favourite restaurant in Seoul sells nothing but kalguksoo (a hot noodle dish) and steamed dumplings. It doesn't just attract locals but also people from distant parts of the country and even foreigners who have read about its reputation. We have to visit this place at least once on every trip we make to Seoul. This restaurant is a good example of a specializing in two different products that complement each other. Some people come for the noodle dish, others for the dumplings; many of both groups end up consuming both dishes.

Sometimes, including several complimentary activities may be mandatory. Selling car tires may well be your core specialization, but you may attract fewer customers if you don't also offer wheel alignment and balancing as services.

Vet Your Core Focus

As with anything in business, test and validate your core focus – especially if it represents a completely new direction in which you have no operational or financial track record of your own to guide you. Consider making prototypes, conducting small-scale trials, or running limited-time promotions to gauge the interest and response from your target audience. Evaluate the feedback and performance of these tests to validate the viability of your chosen specialization.

Your core focus will become a part of your business vision (which we will define in the next chapter) and guide your overall messaging both internally and externally. As such, though we haven't explicitly referred to your business core values in this chapter, your focus should also not in any way conflict with them. If you've chosen "stability" as a key value, for instance, it's probably not a good idea to change your specialization from selling ice cream cones to marketing car parts.

We started the chapter with the quote, "What you stay focused on will grow". "Focus" is the key word here. Attention also needs to be held for it to take root. Once your new core focus has been tested and validated, you must keep a laser-sharp focus on it. It goes without saying that it's much easier to maintain this focus if it forms part of the vision and plan for your business.

Establish Your One-Line Core-Focus Statement

Write down the specialization statement you will from now on refer to in all things you do: marketing, communication, your product offering, hiring process, etc. I am "a small business scale-up specialist". Rachel is "a newborn photography specialist". What is your core focus, and how can you state it comprehensively in just a few words?

Adaptability of Core Focus

"The only constant in life is change." – Heraclitus

As we went through the above process, we selected our specialization with trends and future developments in mind. Customer preferences and technologies will continue to shift, sometimes ever so slightly and gradually and sometimes in a surprisingly rapid way. We will need to stay abreast with and ahead of changes and adapt our offering.

We spoke of some examples of companies that didn't evolve to meet the new digital trends. The current pervasiveness of internet shopping, for example, caught even giant companies by surprise. Their core focus, whether this was selling toys or providing specialized parts to electronics hobbyists, could have stayed the same – if they'd adapted to new realities. We also know some companies that successfully rode the wave, pivoted, and continued to thrive in a changing environment. The best example of this may be Netflix, which started as a rent-by-mail service for DVDs but recognized the shift towards streaming video content in time.

Identifying and understanding trends, then tweaking your offerings to continue staying successful, is key to your sustainable growth. The best way to achieve this is to thoroughly embed this research, interpretation, and adaptation in your business process. Your quarterly vision and goal review meetings should have an agenda item covering trend reviews and adaptation strategies.

Your Action:

Establish Your Core Focus and Get Serious about It – Narrow down your business verticals to those that are most profitable.

A small business can't expect to do everything customers in their industry may desire. Narrowing down what you do, even to a single product line, may increase your market share (of a certain segment) considerably and boost your profitability in numerous ways. There is a structured process to help you determine the best core focus for you.

- Review your current products/service lines both by sales volume and revenue, as well as the costs of delivery. Identify which verticals are most profitable.

- Revise your core focus intentions considering future trends to determine your specialization.

- Vet this decision with prototype trials, market research, etc. and refine it if necessary.

- Establish your one-line specialization statement and make it come alive in your business.

CHAPTER 9

LAUNCHING YOUR AMBITIOUS VISION – THE DRIVER AND FOCUS OF ALL THINGS IN YOUR BUSINESS, YOUR COLLECTIVE DREAMS AND GOALS

"The best way to predict the future is to create it."

– P. Drucker & A. Lincoln, National University

In one of the very first apartments we lived in when we moved to Vancouver from Sweden, the big picture window in my office didn't have a bug screen. So, whenever I'd open the window, I would sometimes be joined by an array of insects. In spring, these were often ladybugs. One morning, I watched one of these crawling back and forth near the same small section of the window frame, trying in vain to get back to the outdoors. This continued for hours until it tired itself out and I stopped the experiment by gently putting it on the sill outside.

Many of us are like this ladybug in one or more aspects of our lives. The choices we make are random instead of being based on a clear plan. We make ineffectual attempts to reach our goals, then get frustrated and discouraged when they don't work. We throw ourselves against barriers again and again instead of zooming out and looking at the big picture. I've seen this time and time again in different contexts, in fact, this could be called the "problem statement" the SCALE-UP system was developed to solve.

Creating a long-term vision for your business simply means determining what you really want. The actual process we are about to embark on is a little more involved, but your true desires lie at its core. Defining your vision encourages you to zoom out, consider what your destination is, and find efficient ways to reach it.

When my clients start working with me, they usually have a fairly non-specific idea of what they would like their company to be someday, at some point in the future. They admit that they've been thinking about opening another branch, or they would like to hit a certain revenue number. However, they have not created a vision that inspires them or their team, nor have they created a plan to achieve that vision.

Just like your personal vision, your business vision provides a destination for any organization. Having a shared business vision brings focus, motivation, and strategic clarity to a company. It guides the whole team toward the kind of future success they desire.

Once you've established this vision, everyone involved in your business will know where you are collectively heading, as opposed to wandering around randomly in the hope of achieving a nebulous goal. In other words, this is how to break free of a ladybug-like cycle of trial and error. In this analogy, you would avoid flying through an open window in the first place. And, if you were to somehow stumble into someone's apartment anyway, your business vision will help you to use a wider perspective to discover the right direction to follow.

Amplify Your Impact

If you've worked in the business world, you will probably have heard of corporate vision statements. For example, Tesla's vision statement is: "To create the most compelling car company of the 21st century by driving the world's transition to electric vehicles." Google's declaration of purpose is: "To provide access to the world's information in one click." You will agree that both companies are actualizing their visions as we speak.

Both of those vision statements are great, and they are certainly powerful. However, what we will be creating during the course of this chapter is more than just a generic explanation of our intentions. As we work through the steps below, we will be creating a compelling, inspiring, and comprehensive picture of where exactly you want to be at some point in the future.

Our starting point will be your business's core strengths: its core purpose, core values, and core focus. Just like, in Chapter 3, we imagined a documentary of your successful future life, we will create a vivid mental image of what business success means to you. In order to do this, we'll break down your vision into different elements, each of which supports all the others to build a thriving business. Dissecting your vision in this way also makes it much easier to involve your whole team in the visioning process and communicate the final result to every one of your business's stakeholders.

One characteristic of every great vision is that it provides a holistic picture, one that goes beyond simple financial goals. It focuses on amplifying the impact your organization has – your core purpose. This impact is what inspires and motivates the growth of your company – in line with its core values. As the business grows, its impact on the community increases and expands, too. In order not to get sidetracked or lose momentum, you as a leader need to ensure your vision remains rooted in what makes your company special and keeps it competitive – your core focus.

In my case, my coaching helps fellow business owners to lead more fulfilling lives through increased productivity. This, paraphrased, is pretty much my own vision statement. Each time I grow my client list, my impact is amplified because I am able to help more business owners. My three business core strengths – my purpose, values, and focus – form an equilateral triangle with my vision in the centre.

Engage Your Team in the Process

Solopreneurs stand or fall on their own. Their personal and business visions tend to be nearly parallel. When you have employees, however, you bear some responsibility for their welfare and fulfillment. Perhaps more importantly, they need to embrace your business vision, or it will not be as effective as it should.

If you have any staff, involve your team members in the visioning process. As discussed in the previous chapters, finding a balance between the business's core strengths and the team's personal core values can be invigorating for everyone involved.

Some companies send out a questionnaire to get everyone's input and later discuss the results within each department. The department heads representing each team then complete the visioning process over one or several meetings. Smaller businesses may gather all employees together, if there aren't too many people to make brainstorming as a group impractical. Which process will work best for you?

Be Aspirational, Inspirational, and Motivating

Set your sights high on creating a vision statement that will inspire you and other stakeholders. In the book *Built to Last: Successful Habits of Visionary Companies*, Jim Collins and Jerry Porras use the phrase "big, hairy, audacious goal", which perfectly captures what a vision should be. It needs to be ambitious and challenging in a way that is exciting and even a little intimidating. The purpose of your vision is to stretch your organization beyond its current capabilities, so it should seem audacious.

Setting big, hairy, audacious goals can inspire and propel an organization to achieve extraordinary results. By aiming for something significant, companies can challenge the status quo and ignite innovation. Once your team is thinking outside the boundaries of what seems possible, new ideas and ways of doing things are bound to turn up. This is very effective way for your vision to unite your team under a common purpose and drive outstanding results.

The status quo is a limit that we create for ourselves based on what other people have achieved in the past. A perfect example of this is the four-minute-mile barrier. For a very long time, running a mile in under four minutes was regarded as humanly impossible. Financial guru Charles M. Schwab said it best: "When we're setting limits to what we can achieve, we're setting limits to what we can achieve!" Tautological, sure, but many profound truths are.

Then, Sir Roger Bannister ran a mile in three minutes and 59.4 seconds in 1954. Suddenly, running a sub-four-minute mile became not only possible but a rite of passage for male middle-distance runners. More than a thousand runners have broken the four-minute barrier to date. Bannister's achievement expanded our perceptions of human potential. A big, hairy, audacious vision does something similar for business owners. It frees us of limits that exist only in our minds so that we can take our businesses to new heights.

Just the way I suggested eight key elements to make a holistic life success vision, I offer five elements for a business vision, demonstrated by this graphic:

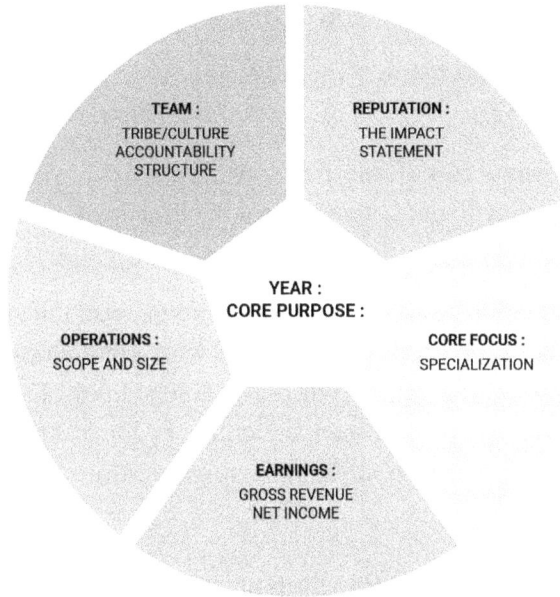

<A Holistic Business Vision>

It helps to have your personal vision statement handy when crafting your business vision. Our aim is to create a business vision that supports your holistically ideal life. When the two vision statements are not in harmony, they can easily end up sabotaging each other.

Choosing an Attainment Date

Just like with your personal vision, you need to pick a future year in which to achieve it. Choosing one that makes sense is more of an art than a science, so don't overthink it. For her vision, my client Rachel chose seven years ahead. This was because that was when her daughter would graduate from high school and her personal vision included her stepping down from her business's day-to-day operations.

Choose a date that is at least five years off. If no particular life event or time-bound business goal comes to mind, ten years from now is far enough away to create an ambitious vision, yet not so distant that your business vision will seem disconnected from daily tasks and decisions.

Build Your Vision

Two things should inspire you during this process:

- **Your personal vision:** Remember that your work vision exists to support your personal one, not the other way around.

- **Your business core strengths:** Core purpose, core values and core focus. These will guide you toward maximizing your enterprise's impact.

Imagine that it's January 1st of the year you chose; take stock of your business. Think of how it feels to go to work, what kind of tasks you occupy yourself with, how conversations with various stakeholders tend to go, and so forth. Once you have a clear mental picture of your company's condition and circumstances, ask yourself the following questions and answer them in the present tense:

Ambitious and Inspiring Reputation

What is one central pillar of the reputation you have created for your business? Be clear, concise, and concrete: clear with your word choices, concise with a sharp focus on your most important attribute, and concrete so that everyone can grasp it. As the heading above says, it should be also inspiring. If what people will be thinking of your company in a few years is not inspiring, it won't motivate you. If you, as the top leader, aren't inspired, you will have a very hard time motivating others.

For example, Rachel wants her business to be the most sought-after photography studio in the Greater Vancouver BC area for pictures of newborn babies. She picked the word "popular" rather than "biggest", "most famous", or "most profitable". Those words would imply a different path for her business, perhaps one that prioritizes quantity over quality. Choose the words that best represent your ambition and resonate with you and your team. An education consultant in one of our previous examples may say "We aspire to be the most reputable college program specialist in Latin America."

Note that both of these examples are also concise and concrete. Neither needs a comma, and both of them tell you exactly what the business wants to be known for.

Offering with a Marked Distinction – Your Core Focus

What products or services does your (future) business offer? Do you have a specialization? Do you have a value proposition significantly different from those of your competition? Are you a one-product specialist outfit or perhaps serve your industry's equivalent of two complementary dishes, like noodles and dumplings? The uniqueness of your offering helps you stand out from the competition, and it's always a crowded marketplace.

I certainly emphasized the benefits of specialization for small businesses in the previous chapter. That being said, I also recognize that not every industry, company, or business owner is too gung-ho about or suited for niching down to a hair's breadth. You may have chosen to be somewhere between a generalist and a specialist. This is fine, but it has to be a conscious, deliberate decision nonetheless.

If I may expand on the hiking analogy once more, it's fair to say that there is often more than one path to your summit of choice. A particular route may be the most efficient way but not one that you'd particularly enjoy taking. After all, you (and your team) will be sweating it out on that path, day in and day out, for years to come. It's best to make sure that you will like the views and can bear the uphill sections.

Now, how do you deliver your offering in a way that makes a difference to those on the receiving end? Remember the kimchi-jjigae restaurant that perfected its style of food service, providing its busy customers not just with fantastic food but also more time for coffee and/or after-lunch walks. What's your irresistible value proposition with your offering?

Your specialized product and the nature of your clientele go hand in hand. Whose lives are you influencing with your offering? How does serving this community support your and your team's fulfillment? What makes customers choose you over the competitor down the street?

Your Top-Line, Bottom-Line, and Take-Home Income

If the words in the heading seem unfamiliar, don't worry: they're just everyday synonyms for more formal accounting terms you probably know.

The top and bottom lines, respectively, refer to your gross revenue and net income. (Take-home income is pretty much self-explanatory.) In your chosen vision year, what size company are you running? We have to establish the scope of your future business because this will play a crucial role in the next steps of the visioning process. If you can, it would be helpful to draw up an imaginary income statement now, containing only the most important of your revenues and expenses.

The difference between your bottom line and your top line, expressed as a percentage, is referred to as your "profit margin". This number is a key financial metric that indicates how efficiently a company is operating and how much profit it generates from each dollar of revenue.

Consider the take-home income required to actualize your holistic life vision. (For simplicity's sake, you don't need to factor in inflation as long as you are considering today's currency for both income and expenses.) Your personal vision and business aspirations will inform what kind of scope to use in your business planning. For example, one of my clients wants their employees to become shareholders in the company, so that will limit the size of their team. In my case, my aspirations include philanthropy, so my plans for charitable contributions add to my business growth goals.

Your Business Operations

What do your future business operations look like? Are you operating in one location or several? Are your clients based locally or all over the world? Do you have branches or franchises? How does your online strategy figure into all of this? Are your employees full-time, part-time, internal, external, remote, or hybrid?

My apologies for throwing this barrage of questions your way all at once. Yet, as you begin to drill down, you'll realize that you can't answer one without thinking about all of them. For instance, if your business model requires your team to work 100% in person, you will need extra floor space. If you choose to offer franchise opportunities instead of keeping all operations in-house, your administrative workload decreases but you'll also have to build entirely new support structures.

Let's use one of my clients, RYP, as an example once more. In its vision year, the business now comprises four branches in total, all of them located in Greater Vancouver. Rachel and her team follow a hybrid working model, sometimes coming into these studios and sometimes working from home. Because their core business is taking photographs of babies, someone will always need to be on location whenever there are photoshoots scheduled. Due to her commitment to quality and customer service, franchising seems like a questionable strategy. If she wanted to expand her operations online (apart from using the internet as a marketing channel), she could perhaps offer to digitally touch up photos parents take themselves. This would distract Rachel and her team from their core focus, however, and therefore plays no part in her envisioned business operations.

Your Team

What is your role in the vision year? Are you involved in daily operations? What kind of individuals find themselves on your team, and what functions does each perform? What leadership and team structure has allowed you to achieve your set aspirations as well as your personal vision?

Returning to RYP, the company has three studio managers plus a general manager who oversees operations in addition to running the fourth studio. Rachel herself, as per her personal vision, only works a few hours each week, focusing on business development and supporting her GM.

In order to deliver your core focus offering with distinction, you will need a team that's not only skilled at the necessary jobs but organized in a way that lets them perform these efficiently. An educational consultancy that specializes in advanced college programs, for example, needs staff with the relevant skill sets. It also requires a more experienced supervisor who's familiar with various fields of study and can pair each student with the right advisor.

Vet Your Vision and Make It Holistic

Each of the vision elements should be harmonious with all the others. In addition, your business vision should dovetail with your personal vision and be compatible with your business's core strengths. If these requirements are all met, you're off to a pretty good start at setting your company on the path to success.

As we did when creating our personal vision, we will now replay your documentary. Chances are that a few scenes have changed based on your more holistic ambitions for your business in the year you chose.

Does everything work in sync or does some part of your vision conflict with the rest? For example, do you claim to be the best kimchi-jjigae restaurant on the block, yet serve twenty other dishes too? Do you say that you're stepping down as boss, yet have no general manager ready to take over? Did you create a sprawling business with only a peripheral connection to your core focus? Does the projected size of your organization match up with your desired take-home income? Do the demands work places on your time take away from your quality of life?

Discrepancies such as these shouldn't be seen as mistakes but as opportunities. The visioning process is inherently iterative: you start with your core strengths (purpose, values, and focus) as a solid base, then keep refining it until you're ready to write a vision statement both you and your team can get excited about. In my case, if my inner documentary showed me that I was making clients feel good about themselves without helping them scale up their businesses in a meaningful way, I'd simply have to adjust one or more of the elements of my vision until they lined up correctly.

Create Your Vision Statement

In year _____,

Our reputation is _____

We offer _____

In this geography, _____

Our delivery is superior because _____

Once you've composed this statement in words that convey your true meaning, jot down a few (private) notes about the high points in your documentary:

_____

3-Year Strategic Goals

Let's return to my hiking hobby. (If you feel that some other activity makes a better metaphor for the journey to fulfillment and success, by all means think in those terms instead.) One of my favourite hiking tracks near our home is nicknamed "The Chief". It is a beautiful trail with spectacular views at the summit. The Chief rises over three peaks in succession, with the third and tallest being the final destination. Cresting the two leading up to it provides milestones. I know I'm on the right track when I have arrived at the first peak.

Your vision, of course, is your destination, your final summit. Your three-year goals are the first peak. Once you reach this, it will lead you on to the second; this marks another milestone you'll pass before getting to your final destination.

These peaks are necessary accomplishments on the way to your goal. Attaining them indicates to you and your team that you are well on your way to achieving your business vision, affirming and reinforcing your collective aspirations. "Yes, we can do it. So far, we have achieved our ambitious goals, so what stops us from achieving the full vision?"

Not passing these milestones on time, on the other hand, signifies that you are not on track to making your business vision a reality. As with

The Chief, there's no clear or easy way to reach the final summit without surmounting the intervening peaks. In other words, part of the visioning process is defining intermediate goals to help us assess our progress.

Establish Your 3-Year Strategic Goals

What do you need to accomplish in the next three years in order to achieve your aspirational vision? We are looking at "big rock" goals here, for those of you who are familiar with the concept. This analogy is based on filling a bucket with dirt: if you pay attention to the most impactful tasks or goals (big rocks) first, you avoid getting bogged down by smaller, less meaningful tasks (sand and pebbles) that would otherwise drain your time and energy.

Determine two to three big goals on the way to fulfilling your vision. Having any more than three may dilute your focus and breed an ever-expanding laundry list of to-dos.

My client RYP's vision is to be the most popular newborn photography business in the Greater Vancouver area. The organization's three strategic goals for the next 36 months are:

1. The successful launch and operation of her second studio. This will demonstrate the business's ability to expand sustainably and profitably. Subsequent expansions will become easier because she'll have a proven blueprint.

2. Establish a strong leader in the first studio. This manager will allow Rachel to focus on the new branch and support her during the expansion. This person will likely also become the general manager at some future point.

3. Establish defined and documented key business processes. This will enable her to efficiently open more studios and operate them productively and profitably.

When RYP achieves these three goals, it will be significantly closer to actualizing its overall vision. Everything will be in place to open her third studio and, in time, her fourth. But she's not quite done yet. It's time to turn these objectives into more granular goals that can be more easily planned for.

Reverse-Engineer Yearly Goals

At this point, you have your business vision more or less nailed down. You also have a few high-level, strategic goals that you want to reach no later than three years from today. It's time to reverse-engineer your three-year goals, breaking them down into yearly goals and eventually actionable items in your calendar.

I find it works best to start with what you want to achieve in Year 3, then work backwards to set targets for Year 2, and finally for the current year. When doing it in the intuitive, chronological, way, we tend to become short-sighted and bogged down in details. It's easy to get lost in the present moment and current challenges. This isn't conducive to strategic thinking, though: any plan made based exclusively on today's realities tends to lack ambition. As they say: "Playing small doesn't serve the world." Your goals have to be aspirational in nature, and they should challenge you. When you work backwards in time, you naturally think bigger.

Let's use RYP's goals as an example again. The S.M.A.R.T. letters are embedded in the goals to indicate that they have passed the SMART framework test.

Year 3

- Yearly (T) gross revenue (S) from the second studio is $250,000 (M) (that is not the real number, as it is confidential). This goal is ambitious but achievable (A) and relevant because it stems from the overall vision (R).

- The yearly (T) overall margin from both studios (S) is 25% (M). Due to the two branches sharing certain costs, the margin has improved (A). This goal also supports the vision (R).

- A complete and repeatable (M) new studio opening process (S) is in place in Q2 (T). It specifies a reasonable timeline and resources (A) and is relevant to the overall vision (R).

Year 2

- A new studio (S) has successfully launched (M) in Q3 (T). This is both feasible and related to the vision (A, R).

- It boasts a yearly (T) gross revenue (S) of $50,000 (M). Again, this is achievable and relevant to the vision (A, R).

Year 1

- The studio manager has completed (M) her first batch of leadership training (S) in a satisfactory manner (M) by the end of the year (T). Achievable and relevant to the vision (A, R).

- The key business processes (S) have been created, completed, documented, audited, and communicated (M) to the team in Q3 (T). Achievable and relevant to the vision (A, R).

- A viable second location (S, M) has been researched and identified by November (T). Achievable and relevant to the vision (A, R).

By spelling out what she needs to have achieved in Year 3, Rachel is able to identify what she can do in Year 2 to put herself in a position to support those goals. The same process is repeated to set targets and actions for Year 1.

Document and Communicate Your Vision and Goals

In business, anything that's not written down may as well not exist, and whatever you don't share with your team will have no effect on their behaviour and decision-making. Document your vision statement, 3-year strategic objectives, and yearly goals and communicate them to the team.

Ideally, of course, all your employees or at least the key players will have worked alongside you throughout the visioning exercise. Your vision, 3-year strategic objectives and yearly goals should reflect their ideas, passions, and expertise. Some people may have been unavailable for some reason, though, and it's very important to convey your vision and goals to new hires.

One of the crucial, but often overlooked, steps in the whole journey of creating a business vision is therefore drafting a template to clarify all the high points. Carefully explain what precisely is envisioned and how you plan to achieve it. Your management team will probably require more detail, though it's a good idea to get the entire staff on board with the new business vision.

You may also choose to include stakeholders outside your business, like your family, if they can offer support, moral or otherwise. They will not only help you in your endeavours where they can but also be an accountability partner to your vision.

My clients who have established their ambitious vision and goals all see greater focus and productivity in their business as a result. Their new, long-term ambition has given their staff the ability to think outside the box and stretch their capabilities. When I first started working with some of my clients as a coach, they wouldn't have dared to contemplate ever being the best in the industry as a small player. Now, armed with their vision, they aspire to be number 1 in their specialized area – audacious indeed!

Establishing your team's summit and major milestones, as long as everyone in your team identifies with them, is a huge motivator and driver when it comes to daily work and short-term planning. I cannot stress enough how important it is to know where we are heading. Equipped with an inspirational business vision, we naturally direct and focus our time and energy on the right things.

Equally importantly, you know what you are saying no to and when this is the right course of action. As I tell my clients: "Saying no comes from empowerment. Saying yes to everything comes from insecurity and a lack of vision." Focusing on the vision leads to greater productivity and, in the long run, thriving communities all around.

Your Action:

Establish Your Ambitious Vision and Direct Your Focus and Energy to It – Create a holistic goal for your business along with a plan to achieve it.

Without a clear vision, any organization tends to amble around aimlessly instead of confidently striding in the right direction. This business vision is based on your core strengths and has to be in harmony with your personal vision statement. Once you know exactly what your business vision is, it's time to take steps to make it a reality.

1. Define your business vision in terms of 5 elements: your reputation, offering, finance, operations, and team.

2. Vet each element to make sure it's harmonious with the rest of the vision, your personal vision, and business core strengths.

3. Create 3-year strategic goals towards your vision.

4. Break them down to Year 3, Year 2, and Year 1 goals, in that order.

5. Document and communicate the above vision and goals with the stakeholders.

6. Most importantly, from here on out, lead your business with this ambitious vision always in mind.

CHAPTER 10

LEADING OTHERS WITH EMPOWERMENT – PULLING TOGETHER TOWARDS YOUR VISION

"Leaders become great not because of their power, but because of their ability to empower others."

– John C. Maxwell

Have you been lucky enough to work directly under a fantastic leader? Have you known (or known about) one you didn't interact with often, yet who still amazed you with their grace, clarity of vision, and charisma? What made you look up to them so much? Leaders are all around us, great, okay, indifferent, bad, or even terrible. Most entrepreneurs learn their leadership style from these examples, both positive and negative.

Leadership changes the course of lives. A good leader can raise everyone to new heights, and a bad leader can derail all enthusiasm and productivity. This impact, for better or worse, is felt by everyone involved and sticks around for a long time. Good leaders elevate others, themselves, and the organization as a whole. Bad ones do the exact opposite – possibly without even realizing what effect they're having!

This is why I am so passionate about leadership. I have seen firsthand what can be achieved through good leadership and how bad leadership can leave trails of destruction in its wake. It is impossible to cover everything I would like to tell you about leadership in one chapter, so we'll focus on the leadership characteristics that are essential for scaling up a small business.

Leader, Lead Thyself

Part I of this book gave you a strong foundation of self-leadership to build upon. When you know your life purpose, core values, vision, and goals, and have implemented a productivity system that enables you to put these into practice, you're much closer to knowing who you are. This self-knowledge, in turn, makes you much more decisive and effective as a leader.

Once we as entrepreneurs have scaled up ourselves, we can scale up our business much more efficiently. Let's return to the images we reflected on in the introduction to Part I: one of a small stick figure confronted with a gigantic boulder, and another of a much bigger figure in front of the same boulder. These represent the same person, but the figuratively bigger person, having grown themselves, can step over the obstacle with ease and grace.

This is an important concept. Without knowing how to manage yourself strategically in order to actualize your vision of success, it is unlikely that you'll be able to effectively lead others. This lack of self-knowledge and self-leadership results in all kinds of absurd situations.

Have you ever seen a leader preach timeliness and criticize their team for being tardy when they are often late themselves? Or one who constantly complains about their team's lack of commitment yet shows little dedication to either their responsibilities or their team? It is hard to take a leader seriously when they are not walking their talk. Their actions show that they are not aligned with what they preach, so why would their team pay attention to what they say?

Actions, especially consistent actions, speak louder than words. Aside from the benefits of leading by example, what you say carries more weight when you walk your talk. When you are focused on what matters, it gives clear signals to your stakeholders about what is important for your business to succeed. This also provides a powerful lesson concerning how to be successful within the organization, which automatically encourages the behaviours you're trying to foster. Your business should be a vehicle for the success of your employees as much as it is a way for you to achieve your life vision. It all starts with abandoning the "do as I say, not as I do" mentality. In a small business, greatness starts at the very top with the owner.

With your self-leadership well established, you're in a much better position to lead your stakeholders according to the same principles. The next section offers advice on how you can lead those around you to their wins, thereby achieving corresponding wins for your business. The guiding principles below will underpin empowerment for all involved and bolster your business's success.

Embrace a Win-Win Mindset

One character trait of great business leaders is that they guide all stakeholders to achieve more. You can do this by cultivating a mindset that looks for mutually beneficial solutions and opportunities – all the time.

One of my clients, during the portion of my coaching that deals with leadership, asked me to look over a complaint they recently received and asked how they should handle similar situations in the future. A customer, after the service had been rendered, expressed unhappiness with the communication and demanded a refund. This organization had a policy, like many service providers, that refunds were not possible after their part of the contract had been completed. Still, the customer was dissatisfied, citing the way they were treated by a particular staff member. My client was eager to hear my recommendations on how to handle these kinds of situations.

As I mentioned in Chapter 7, on core values, the most difficult decisions tend to be those that involve people. In this case, my client had to consider her obligations to three stakeholders: the customer, the employee in question, and the business itself. There is no one right way to handle this scenario – it will differ from situation to situation and organization to organization. So, I asked this client questions to determine what the ideal outcome would be for their organization (a win for the business). The client stated:

- Being able to keep the money instead of refunding or partially refunding the customer.

- Having a happy customer.

- Having an employee who feels heard and supported (instead of feeling like they were undermined or thrown under the bus just to keep the customer happy).

Then, I asked what the desired outcome for the customer (win for the customer) would be. The client thought for a moment and said:

- Getting a full or partial refund.

- Getting an apology.

- Having the business troubleshoot why the service didn't achieve the desired outcomes.

When a leader approaches conflict (or, in fact, any conversation) with an understanding of what each party would consider a win, they are already that much closer to finding a win-win resolution. In this example, that may mean nothing more than the employee giving a sincere apology that acknowledges their poor choice of words. This would show that the organization took the customer's complaint seriously and that it truly wants the best for its customers.

The business owner shared with me later that they did respond to the customer's complaint in a timely manner. After talking to the employee, they agreed that she would apologize. The customer was also given a credit that they or a friend could use with the business for 20% of the value of their original purchase. The customer was extremely pleased with this solution and said he would definitely return to the business.

So far, we have created a win for the customer and a win for the organization by creating a happy customer and possibly returning business. How about a win for the staff involved? In my leadership coaching, "conversations worth having" is a recurring topic. Often, leaders avoid and postpone important dialogues in an effort not to upset their staff or because they're uncomfortable with confrontation. Many just don't know how to lead effective conversations when the issues under discussion may create tension and agitate some people. More than a few are afraid that calling someone out may lower overall staff morale and performance.

For any of the reasons above, my client could also have chosen not to involve the employee responsible and apologized on behalf of the organization instead. This solution would probably have satisfied the customer; however, the same staff member may continue to cause similar incidents in the future. Even worse, not addressing the matter with the teammate may quietly and unintentionally communicate to the rest of the team that poor communication or service will be tolerated by management. As such, this "solution" didn't create a win for the staff or the organization.

The potential win for the staff here lies in the area of professional development and represents a growth opportunity. I will share an example from another of my clients, Gabi, later in this chapter to demonstrate how leaders can commit to their team's growth and development while pursuing business wins.

In this case, the employee could benefit from being coached on ways to improve her communication. How do we have a conversation that is not only respectful of our customers (or whatever other stakeholders may be involved in the situation) but also perceived as supportive by the employee? The conversation worth having, in this case, is a helpful, instructive one where the leader asks the team member in what ways her future conversations with customers might go differently under similar circumstances. When this dialogue – and it should be a dialogue, not a sermon – is framed in win-win terms, it empowers the employee to be more confident in her future interactions not only with customers but also in her personal life.

In this situation and others, it is highly likely that all parties perceive potential wins in different ways. Their interests will rarely be identical, but that doesn't mean they have to be completely divergent. The best we can do is to truly listen and ask questions in order to understand everybody's perspectives and try to create wins all around. Win-win is a mindset, it is not an achievable outcome in for every situation.

Ensure Long-Term Wins

When we create wins for multiple stakeholders, we always want to consider the long game. In fact, I would go as far as saying that the win-win mindset implies embracing a long-term perspective. From now on, make a point of asking yourself: "What outcome would ensure a long-term win for everybody involved?"

Before becoming a professional business coach, I used to work in sales and marketing. On one occasion, some of our wholesalers agreed to receive a lower commission than their counterparts who ordered an equal or lower volume of products each year. We'd sometimes agree to a higher rate only when a particular partner forced the issue. This seemed like a good outcome for us in the short term: we paid less commission and we assumed that the wholesalers who didn't complain were happy with the lower rate.

Was this truly a win-win situation, though? Not likely! And certainly not in the long term. Inequitable partnerships are unlikely to last long. As soon as the other party found a better deal elsewhere (or worse, found out that other wholesalers were getting higher commissions from us), they would switch suppliers. In this case, since we chose to re-negotiate our arrangements specifically with high-volume wholesalers, this drop in customer loyalty hurt us particularly badly.

The same applies to salary negotiations with employees. There are dozens if not hundreds of jokes about employers demanding above-average work for substandard pay. Offering lower wages may, at first, seem like a better "deal" for your business. However, talented individuals who know their worth are unlikely to hang around for long. Conversely, when valuable employees are well taken care of in terms of developmental opportunities, financial remuneration, and other factors (like their personal core values aligning with those of the company), they are likely to stay for a long time while remaining committed and productive.

How about your clients? Ensuring their long-term wins is very likely to bring you long-term success. Ultimately, lasting partnerships benefit both you and them. It is costly – in time, energy, and money – to recruit new employees, clients and wholesalers, so each long-term win-win partnership you establish greases your success wheel.

Communicate to Connect

In *The 7 Habits of Highly Effective People*, Stephen Covey has an entire chapter on "Seek to Understand" as opposed to "listening to respond". This is sage advice.

Not only does this allow us to understand the other person's perspective better (which is necessary to create a win-win outcome), it makes the other person feel heard – the beginning of any meaningful connection. We have all experienced the opposite: the hearers who are just waiting to respond and not actually listening to what you are saying. It is unlikely you felt that person was someone you could trust or even someone you wanted to talk to more often. This communicator just lost an opportunity to connect and build trust.

I like to encourage leaders to take "listening to understand" one step further and "listen to connect". We can either connect and build trust or disconnect and build barriers, and a lot of which you choose depends on your approach to communication. Business is social: we conduct it with people, for people, and through people. If we don't connect with the people involved, success will remain an illusion. Communicating to connect focuses us on the quality of communication with the intent to listen fully and create a win-win.

Intention doesn't always equal action. This is what I witness in myself and others. That's why I encourage leaders to plan their connections with important stakeholders. Who do you need to connect with regularly? How often should you connect? Schedule those meetings in your calendar. Now, your hope can become reality.

In business, the most important connection of all is with your team – both collectively and individually. Of all the stakeholders you interact with, your staff has the greatest influence on your success. I've seen the benefits of my clients communicating regularly with their teams. They have weekly staff meetings to review progress and set priorities for the week, they have project meetings, and they train as a team. These meetings are important in unblocking challenges and synergistically pursuing opportunities.

Something that's a little more rare is regularly scheduled one-on-one meetings with all your direct reports. With these, the primary goal is to connect and build a strong rapport with each other, face to face. Consider your staff the most essential asset for your scale-up and the actualization of your vision. I have a bit more information about how to do this in Chapter 13, Establishing Processes of Success.

It is easy for these inclusive one-to-one meetings to fall by the wayside. Given the demands of day-to-day activities, leaders may prioritize "business" over the people who make it possible or clients over employees. You may believe that team members will bring urgent issues to your attention. Some may, but this reactive approach is missing the point of one-on-ones.

Your staff is the most important asset in your business. You need to know what is going on in their lives, both at work and at home. Why would you be interested in their personal lives? Because our work effectiveness can be severely hampered when our personal lives suffer. If you're able to build enough trust and your staff is willing to discuss their private matters, you can provide assistance in whichever way helps. Even moral and emotional support can mean a great deal in certain situations.

What other regular opportunities can you create to connect with your stakeholders? You may establish regular one-on-one meetings or calls with your clients to quickly check-in and address any budding issues. You will, naturally, already have your business meetings scheduled but may not have "intent to connect" meetings established just yet. These can even be incorporated into your already-established meetings, if you intend to spend the first five to ten minutes just deepening your rapport with the person in front of you.

You will be surprised at the kinds of bonds you'll build and how far this goes in your business. Communicating to connect not only benefits your company but also has the additional advantage of satisfying our deeply human need for connection and belonging. When I was travelling around the world in my role as chief marketing officer, I would spend the first meetings with my clients purely on getting to know each other, with very little talk about our business dealings. This seemed surprising to both the clients and my sales team accompanying me. Doing so may seem unorthodox, but I've found that identifying with one another on a deeper level and agreeing on our common purpose of serving our community made the business part so much smoother and more fun.

Another element of effective communication was already mentioned above but is worth touching on again, and that is frequency. Poor quality communication can result in all kinds of misunderstandings and misalignment, and is often simply the result of not getting in touch often enough. Your team members or clients no longer know your perspective, so they work from the only perspective available to them – their own.

Avoiding this state of affairs means paying attention to both the quality and quantity of communication. In order to ensure that we communicate with our staff frequently enough, we can create regular pre-scheduled meetings (i.e. one-to-ones) weekly. This is further detailed in Chapter 13, Processes of success, later in this book.

Misunderstandings and misinterpretations can still happen, even when we communicate with the intent to listen fully, create a win-win mindset, and talk as frequently as necessary. When we don't even try, however, we are just increasing the opportunities for misalignment and decreasing the opportunity to connect.

Accountability as Your Middle Name

U. S. President Harry Truman, widely regarded as an exceptional leader, famously kept a sign saying: "The Buck Stops Here" on his desk. In essence, he was saying that he accepted responsibility, though not necessarily blame, for anything anybody who worked for him might do.

Effective business leaders have to embrace accountability across all functions and operations. This principle forms part of their systems and the way they conduct their business. True accountability is achieved only once we have set our goals and measurements. In a Chapter 13 in Part III, we discuss how to build accountability into our organizational structure and systems.

Many business owners express their resentment at the fact that their employees aren't performing as well as they'd like. Surprisingly often, the cause lies with the owners themselves. They simply haven't set shared expectations with their staff, who are not mind readers.

You can't, for instance, just tell your head of marketing that they are now responsible for all marketing operations. What does that even mean? Left to their own devices, your head of marketing will determine their role in terms of whatever makes sense from their own perspective. What they come up with will probably not be what you would have meant, had you actually expressed it in words.

Setting clear expectations, on the other hand, clarifies the result you want to achieve in the marketing sphere in definite, measurable terms. For example, your head of marketing may be responsible for generating high-quality leads (as defined by the organization). You would hold this person accountable for generating a specific number of leads per week or month. Your head of marketing can then turn these metrics into goals for their team and, in turn, hold them responsible for meeting those.

Regularly reviewing and discussing these metrics in one-to-one meetings will help you assess performance and identify areas of success and areas where improvements can be made. This can be an opportunity for everyone involved to grow both personally and professionally. In my experience, every person wants to expand their capabilities and better themselves.

In fact, accountability is one of the reasons that my clients seek out coaching in the first place. Everyone up and down their organizational hierarchy has someone above them to hold them accountable and steer them in the right direction if necessary. But who does the same for the business's owner, especially when it comes to their big aspirations?

Knowing that accountability is important is one thing. You may have even chosen it, or a closely related concept, as one of your business's core values. Embodying this principle in our daily business activity, however, requires an active effort and some planning. How do you hold everyone accountable for fulfilling their roles and achieving their goals?

Leaders are expected to set the same standard for both themselves and their team and then hold everyone accountable to those benchmarks. Unfortunately, I have seen plenty of examples of how leaders can get this wrong. Some entrepreneurs and managers hold everyone to a much higher standard than they can maintain themselves. Others do the opposite – expecting immense dedication from themselves but cutting their employees excessive slack.

Earlier in this chapter, we looked at what happens in the first scenario. When you fail to walk your talk, you're seen as a hypocrite and your words will not carry any weight with your team. The second kind of situation is actually more common with business owners. Sometimes, they prefer to avoid the tension inherent in reprimanding a subordinate and instead focus on their daily activities, getting things done but ignoring a larger problem. Instead of addressing an individual's under-achievement, they might dismiss the situation as a one-off case in which the staff member just "dropped the ball". When this reoccurs, they vainly hope that the employee will "learn and change" one day. However, looked at objectively, we know this won't happen by itself. What is needed is a "conversation worth having" to rectify the situation as painlessly as possible.

When we first met, one of my clients, Gabi, would describe herself as "too kind" when talking about the kind of boss she was. I don't believe there is such a thing as too kind. So, after digging a little deeper, Gabi expressed her frustration with herself over her inaction regarding underperforming team members. Her "kindness" was getting in the way of her being an effective leader.

She was falling into a trap that many leaders fall victim to. They dread creating tension within the team and may be afraid of lowering everyone's morale, hence avoid putting their foot down. Perhaps they themselves have had a bad experience when they were held accountable in a way that felt unkind or unfair.

Accountability is not inherently unkind, though. In fact, holding someone accountable for their actions can be the kindest thing you can do for them, as well as providing a tool for personal empowerment. People naturally want to contribute and deliver, and when they succeed in their roles, they feel fulfilled. If they are not performing up to par, they'd probably prefer knowing and being given a chance to improve rather than remaining unsure of how well they're doing. Most likely, they already know intuitively that they're not living up to expectations, and that's not a great feeling.

When we look at accountability from this angle, isn't it more unkind to hope that people will somehow just do better by themselves without being given the necessary help and guidance? How will your staff members feel when they realize that they are constantly falling short of expectations, see their mistakes turning into bigger and bigger problems, and all the while their leader is pretending that the situation doesn't exist?

In Gabi's situation, we looked at the optimum outcomes for every stakeholder.

- What would a win look like for the employee who is becoming a burden to their teammates?

- What would a win look like for the rest of the team?

- What would a win look like for her business?

- What would a win look like for Gabi herself?

Gabi's inherent kindness is not what needs to change – that is who she is; her authentic self. She just needed to determine how she could be kind while also being effective as a leader. As humans, we often seek the path of least resistance so, of course, bosses who offer easy rides are popular. However, a popular boss is not the same as a competent one. Given the choice, most talented, hardworking employees would prefer to work for the latter kind.

While coaching Gabi, she and I explored a new leadership approach she could follow, one that would ensure multiple wins for all stakeholders. As part of this, we tried to see if there was a word that could replace "kind" in her thinking.

Gabi redefined her role as leader as: helping all of her reports to be their best selves, in their best roles, while contributing to the business's success and therefore feeling valued. Armed with this new mindset – similar to but also distinct from her old, narrower concept of "kindness" - she firmly established her leadership anew.

From the perspective of being supportive of each team member's success, she looked at employees who were not pulling their own weight as those who wanted to be accountable, yet were not able to in their current roles. Thinking back to Jim Collins's bus analogy, they may not be in the right seats (possess the right skill set for their roles), or they might not be the right people (have the right cultural fit for the business.)

Gabi established clear guidelines of what was expected of the team and began to hold them accountable. She established regular meetings where she could connect with everybody, one-on-one. The team now felt supported and empowered because they knew exactly how to succeed in their roles and had the opportunity to receive help and guidance from Gabi. Some team members, regrettably, had to go as they weren't a good fit. Though this was painful in the short term, that was still a positive outcome for all involved, as they were now able to look for a better fit for their skills and qualities.

Accountability doesn't just apply to those below us in the company hierarchy. Leaders also need to be part of the accountability system. When Gabi became a supportive leader, she set clear expectations and held every-one accountable to these standards. This includes herself, and this fact is visible to everyone. Now, any problems with performance are being actively addressed and problems solved proactively.

Lead with a Shared Vision

People think that visionary leaders are simply born that way, but that's completely untrue. We're all born with the potential to be visionary leaders – what we need is a vision for us and others to strive for. As it happens, you created an ambitious and inspiring vision for your business in the previous chapter.

A visionary leader is someone who leads people according to an inspiring vision, helping them to do incredible things and unlock new potential. This ability is within the grasp of every leader.

The first step, not surprisingly, is to have an ambitious business vision. The second is to share that vision with your team. The third is to lead using that vision at every opportunity. Bake the purpose, values, and focus on which your vision is based into all of your targets and accountability systems. Frequently remind your team of what you are collectively trying to achieve. In Part III, we will establish this as part of your business system.

Focus Is Your Mantra

Any business today, from the most cutting-edge to the most traditional, operates in a constantly changing environment. This presents a myriad of challenges, but it also brings with it a treasure trove of opportunities. Both the challenges and opportunities can sidetrack us in different ways, distracting us from our core business focus. Regardless, the guiding star that always deserves and requires the greatest attention and commitment is the vision you share with your team. "What you focus on grows." Ensure that the team's focus is on the business vision and its related goals.

Fluctuating market conditions, changing consumer trends, and new innovations mean that we need to be aware of what is going on around us and, at times, adapt to new circumstances. Doing so should never be at the expense of your focus on your vision, though, even if the means to that end change. Focus is what creates productivity – not in the sense of being as busy as possible, but rather according to my definition of spending your energy where it matters.

Gardening is a hobby of mine, and I think tending to plants is very similar to growing a business. You start by planting a seed, with big dreams of what it will grow into. However, it takes time for that plant to germinate, take root, and flourish. For the first few days or weeks, you will be nurturing that seed with no indication of whether or not your efforts will one day bear fruit. When the shoots are finally visible, it is a huge relief to see a sign that your efforts are paying off, but the work is far from over. You still have years ahead of you during which the plant will need to be guarded and pruned to bloom into everything you envisioned it to be.

With focus, the seed you're planting today will be cared for and eventually become a beautiful fruit tree that yields an abundant harvest. It will not, if you allow yourself to succumb to the "shiny object" syndrome. This is a common ailment among entrepreneurs: abandoning your current project in favour of chasing after some other idea, business model, or market.

The problem with shiny object syndrome is that there is never a shortage of new ideas, new tools, and new processes. One of my clients has shiny object syndrome and is constantly bringing new platforms as well as new ideas to his team – to their dismay. Again, this is a common failing among entrepreneurs and other instinctive innovators. They see opportunities everywhere. They skip from one business idea to another, from one potential product to another, from one marketing avenue to another. This results in a lack of focus, leading to a loss of productivity and exhausting everyone involved. Having worked with many business leaders, I know that a lack of productivity is usually the result of a lack of focus. When we don't know where we are heading, we tend to wander. Your lack of focus can also have a contagious effect on your team members, especially if you don't regularly reinforce the business vision in their minds.

I like to think of myself as particularly focused. However, I also struggle not to get distracted by new ideas. What grounds me when I get excited about a new concept is to refer back to my vision. I consider which ideas support my vision and whether I have given my current ideas enough time to sprout and grow. We all have only a finite amount of time, so when we say yes to something, it means saying no to something else. Taking on a new idea means rejecting something we are currently focusing on. In most cases (though not all) your vision will be best served by sticking to the project in which you've already invested considerable time and effort.

Become a People-Gardener, a.k.a. a "Chief Growth Officer" (CGO)

Recently, I noticed a certain theme coming up time and time again in my conversations with one particular client. That theme could be summed up in one word: control. My client was asking: "How can I control my team's work?" He felt like he couldn't trust his employees to fulfill their responsibilities without him breathing down their necks to a way greater extent than accountability requires.

Frustrated, he asked me: "How can I create a team committed to doing their work when I'm not around?"

Another client of mine recently discovered that some of her team members weren't putting in the hours they were supposed to. She asked: "How can I hire and retain a more dedicated team?"

Another business owner was frustrated that his staff was producing reports that weren't meeting his expectations. What a waste of time, for both him and them!

All the business owners above are from different industries, yet they all claim to have the same problem: "people". I respectfully disagree. "People" are not the problem; a lack of commitment and team spirit is. A desire to be valued and the ability to commit to a greater cause are both qualities inherent to most adults. Pretty generally, a lack of commitment stems from a lack of alignment.

If employees' personal aspirations are not being honoured in their current workplace or there is a cultural disconnect between them and their employer, they will feel no or little commitment toward the team. Another, related, possibility is that they're experiencing a lack of leadership and accountability, so they don't know what's expected of them. Either way, a motive force or a directing influence is missing from their lives at work. Regardless of their good intentions, desire to be part of the team, and willingness to help achieve business success, people in this position aren't going to hold much passion for their current job.

In the example of my first client, he is worried about some staff not getting their tasks completed in a timely manner unless they're constantly urged onward. Imagine, instead, that they each had strong feelings of ownership of their work. In this case, encouragement from their boss would be superfluous: being fully dedicated to their tasks would come naturally because their individual and shared successes would bring them fulfillment and advance their personal vision. Naturally, they would act differently than they did before.

The second example is similar. Her employees were leaving work much earlier than they should even though they had clear weekly targets to meet. The client's initial solution was to put a system in place to give her greater control over their hours and attendance. This, to me, is like treating a brain tumour with a headache pill. Instead, what if each and every staff member is committed to achieving their respective goals because doing so will make them feel more fulfilled, both professionally and personally? If this were the case, they'd also automatically care much more about their team and the company as a whole. Should any of the team members fall short of their goals, the rest would be inclined to pick up the slack instead of sauntering out the door at 5 p.m. sharp.

The third example concerns colleagues who don't produce quality reports. How likely do you think it is that an employee wants to spend hours preparing paperwork that doesn't actually give their boss the information he needs? A more probable scenario is that team members lack adequate training or clear instructions as to what exactly the report should contain. The moral that binds these three stories together is clear: when a task and the person who is performing it have the right alignments of guidance, skills, and motivation, many of these kinds of frustrations are smoothly avoided.

Though the "people" problems these entrepreneurs each identified seem unconnected, we have a common diagnosis (lack of alignment) for all of them. The good news is that there's a straightforward prescription – find and build this alignment. A good boss knows that one of the most crucial parts of their role is to hire and develop their employees. Their success within the organization is reflected in that of their leader.

One factor which may take you from a good boss to a superb leader is caring about their success beyond the organization, too. Some of your employees will, no doubt, move on from your company one day. Your goal isn't to make them stay forever; instead, you should try to ensure that their personal aspirations are met through their employment with you, however long that may last. Doing this encourages alignment between them and the business, guaranteeing their commitment to their job at your organization along with exceptional performance. It's also a major draw for talented new employees. Which would you rather see in your benefits package: an extra week's vacation or guidance that can accelerate your career path by years?

I recommend my "Personal Growth Program" to all of my clients; it's specifically designed for leaders who want to be "Chief Growth Officers" and become more than a boss to their staff. I strongly suggest that you consider doing this, especially if your team currently seems to be lacking commitment. In the next chapter, on building elite teams, I will introduce this concept in more detail, as well as provide a template that you can use to support better alignment between business goals and employee fulfillment.

Show Up as a Leader, Always – Your Leadership Presence

Being a leader starts with owning the role. That means bringing the qualities of leadership to all the things you do, whether that be team meetings, client conversations, or marketing decisions. A stranger wandering in shouldn't have any doubts as to who is in charge. Lead each conversation you have, tactfully or directly, toward creating winning outcomes for all. In other words, you will always approach each problem with the goal of ensuring success for everyone, as well as taking responsibility for making this happen.

It all starts by embracing the mantle of leadership. This is essentially nothing more than an attitude. You don't have to change your habits, forget your manners, or wear only suits from now on. You also don't have to assign yourself a fancy job description, insist that people call you "ma'am" or "sir", or purchase a megaphone. These and similar outward expressions of dominance can even be warning signs of insecure, weak leaders with neither a clear vision nor the respect of their teams. Great leaders don't rely on such tricks; their leadership qualities are all internal and more subtle.

Have you seen leaders who basically invisible? They tend to use their titles to accomplish the heavy lifting and try to free-ride without ever actually leading or taking responsibility. In their case, The Buck Stops Elsewhere. On the other hand, you may have experienced (and maybe even were) one of those people who can command a room with their leadership presence, with or without an official title. They lead by being passionate and assertive sometimes, often by uplifting a colleague in despair, and often without saying a word but just by being fully present.

As you start thinking about what leadership means to you, make sure to remember that it cannot exist without followership. It is also most effective when followers understand the benefits of seeing you as their leader. These may include inspiration, vision, being part of a winning team, career development, accountability at all levels, security, support, consideration for their needs and values, and respect for their skills and knowledge. Looking back at the previous sentence, which of those benefits wouldn't increase employee engagement and productivity?

Clients, employees and all stakeholders will see that you can lead them to success through creating win-win scenarios, whatever your products and services. You will never see the same kind of loyalty if you merely pursue your own success or simply pay lip service to virtues like connection, understanding, and mutual benefit. A lack of personal or professional integrity is extremely detrimental to effective leadership – and not at all hard to spot. A leader who succeeds at the expense of their subordinates, for instance, can expect to run out of followers pretty quickly.

Always bring a mental outlook appropriate to leadership to all things you do, from one-on-one meetings with employees to strategic planning sessions. Whether you are leading from the front, side, or rear, it's up to you to guide conversations to a winning outcome for everyone. The question authentic leaders always ask themselves is: "How do we win – collectively?" In other words: "How do we create success for everyone, not just the guy in charge?"

Your Action:

Lead, Always! – Understand that leadership begins with accountability, is driven by vision, and functions largely through effective communication.

Good leadership starts with self-knowledge, including knowing your purpose, values, and vision. Effective leaders tend to be those who always look for long-term, win-win outcomes. As a means to this end, they learn to be active communicators (in terms of both connection and frequency) as well as good listeners, and always use their vision to guide and inspire both themselves and others.

1. Take stock of your leadership essentials

   - Win-win, long-term mindset

   - Communicate to connect

   - Lead with a shared vision

   - Focus as your mantra

   - Become a "Chief Growth Specialist"

   - Always lead

2. Designate one area in which you can grow to make a significant difference to your leadership effectiveness.

3. Schedule a list of S.M.A.R.T. actions to improve in your growth area.

CHAPTER 11

DESIGNING YOUR ELITE TEAM – WORK IN UNISON TO DELIVER YOUR VISION

"A team aligned behind a vision will move mountains."

– Kevin Rose, American internet entrepreneur

I've been working with small business owners and leaders for the past few decades. One of the common themes I've noticed during this time is how their biggest challenges (and opportunities) all involve people, and specifically their workforce.

In almost any kind of business, the biggest rewards await us when our people thrive; equally, the biggest risk to our growth is that employees end up feeling unfulfilled and dissatisfied. When this happens, it's almost inevitable that they'll stray from the business vision, start working at cross-purposes, and eventually leave for greener pastures (i.e. a company that offers greater alignment with their goals and core values). This is why building a strong, cohesive team is absolutely essential for any business that wants to grow and scale. A one-person operation can be profitable – to an extent. It can certainly support the owner's lifestyle. Those who want to grow their impact beyond that, and perhaps downsize their own role eventually, need a team.

If you have an ambitious vision for your ideal lifestyle, achieving it will require more people than just yourself. You will need to form an elite team, though this doesn't have to mean salaried employees: the people who help you actualize your vision may be part of your organization, external to it, or some combination of these. Whatever staffing model is most suited to your circumstances, your elite team must be specifically built to deliver your vision. This implies that each individual belongs to the right culture, has the right skills and qualities for their roles, and is able to deliver exceptional teamwork. Together, your elite team can achieve extraordinary results – move mountains, as the quote above says.

Like an orchestra that creates beautiful music through synchronized collaboration, an elite team exceeds expectations by leveraging the unique talents of each of its members, harmonizing their efforts, and working towards a shared vision.

Depending on your business model, your optimal elite team may take the form of a traditional organization structured around employees, supervisors, and managers, or it may be a system of external vendors and contractors supporting a one-person operation. The advice in this chapter remains applicable either way, though the content may be geared more towards companies that rely on internal teams.

"Elite", in the sense used in this book, refers primarily to individual talents in each role. We need each member of our team to be top-notch, not settle for a few superstars backed up by a group of serial bunglers. Imagine an organization that's able to generate great, qualified leads but fails to convert those opportunities into sales. Or a business with both great leads and strong salespeople to convert those customers, but which can't deliver consistent service. All it takes is one underperforming department or division to derail all progress and ultimately bring the whole business down.

The best analogy for a strong team is a smoothly synchronized orchestra. In an orchestra, each member plays a different instrument and melody, thus makes a unique contribution to the overall performance. Similarly, in an elite team, each individual supplies their own expertise, skills, and perspectives, working in harmony toward a common business goal.

In an orchestra, the conductor acts as the leader, guiding and coordinating the efforts of the musicians. They set the tempo, ensure everyone is in sync, point out areas for improvement, and generally bring out the best in each performer. Conductors are remarkably aware of each individual contributor. It's fascinating to see them constantly zero in on different sections and performers to deliver instructions and encouragement. Likewise, in an elite team, a capable leader provides direction, fosters collaboration, and ensures that everyone is orientated towards achieving a common vision.

Just like the musicians in an orchestra, team members in an elite team have a profound understanding of their respective roles and responsibilities. They communicate effectively, actively listen to one another, and seamlessly coordinate their efforts. Each member knows when to take the lead and when to play a supporting role, just like musicians who take turns with solos and harmonies.

Before even making it into an orchestra, each musician will have practised and rehearsed extensively to hone their individual skills. Being a solo virtuoso isn't enough, though: they spend hours each week practising as a group to achieve precision and harmony. Similarly, an elite team invests time in training, learning, and developing their combined skills, ensuring a high level of proficiency and adaptability.

Ultimately, again like an orchestra that creates beautiful music through synchronized collaboration, an elite team achieves remarkable results by leveraging the unique talents of its members, harmonizing their efforts, and working towards a shared vision. Clearly, each employee, especially those in key roles, needs to have a solid skill set as individuals. In order to allow them to truly shine, though, they and their colleagues require a well-thought-out framework within which to operate.

Designing an Elite Team

Your business vision dictates the skills and qualities the elite team you will build needs to incorporate. This may sound counter-intuitive, but building an elite team doesn't start with your current team as a baseline. In small businesses, we can get very attached to our individual staff members because we work so closely with them, and this attachment often limits our perception and scope. Think of it this way: if you wanted to create a sports car, you probably wouldn't do so by modifying a farm tractor.

Working from the opposite end, i.e. starting at the finish line, is a much more efficient way of designing the best team. This approach frees you from being strait-jacketed by current realities. When drawing up a blueprint, it's best to start with a blank slate. This lets you design the most efficient team structure, including the relevant skill sets and qualities for each role, without being distracted by current team members. This process empowers and grows both the business and its employees: though some may see their positions become obsolete at some point in the future, both they and those with a place in the new organization will have the opportunity to move to roles where they can make a greater impact.

Let's take a look at an example. A certain company is currently operating only in Canada. Its vision is to establish a presence in Australia as well as the United States in the next five years. Starting with their vision and strategic goals allows the leaders to identify the right team structure. Clearly, the organization needs to add Australian and American market-specific sales expertise, among other things. They already have Canadian experts to serve the Canadian vertical. The staff with Australian and American experience could come from their ranks, though they'll most likely have to recruit others from external sources.

The latter point is often an uncomfortable one, as it may seem as if loyal Canadian sales and marketing staff will have to be sidelined instead of promoted, even as the company they've served for years is expanding. This fear underpins a tendency that I see quite often: trying to build the vision with the current team in mind. At best, this limits a leader's scope of action when trying to achieve their vision. Even if they have ambitious goals, using the current team and structure has a few pitfalls:

- The business hasn't fully established the skill sets required to deliver the vision because they are constrained by the current team's abilities. This situation is made worse if the company does not have a concrete development plan to narrow the gap. The status quo continues and will only lead to a status quo business that's poorly suited to pursue new opportunities or adapt to emerging trends.

- Without a proper gap analysis and development plan, the current team often gets stretched thin, with more skilled employees gradually taking on more and more responsibilities while others get left behind. This results in substandard productivity for both those with valuable expertise and others trying to acquire new knowledge without their leader's support.

- Team members aren't able to benefit from "new blood": outside hires with expertise and viewpoints that can energize the team and expand everyone's overall skill sets.

- When most employees are used to just doing their jobs within the status quo, adaptability and innovation can be stifled. This negatively affects the momentum needed for an ambitious vision, so any scale-up will be slower than it needs to be.

Even if your current staff and organizational structure function adequately, they may not be suited to the challenges to come. The objective in designing an elite team is not, however, to push out employees who may already be committed to and well-aligned with the business vision. Retaining, retraining, and possibly repurposing some of them isn't an aspect of the plan we need to worry about right now, though. For the moment, we have to think conceptually rather than practically, in terms of what should be rather than what is.

1. Design Your Team Structure

You may have noticed that each component of the SCALE-UP system dovetails neatly with the others. The process for planning your elite team's organization is no different in this respect. In this case, we will use your 3-year strategic goals, which are based on your overall business vision, as a starting point.

While reviewing these goals, make a list of the skill sets required to accomplish them at a macro level. You don't need to get too specific; you may, for example, write down "website designer" instead of "front-end PHP developer". It's helpful to imagine that it's already the end of Year 3 and see which skill sets have been put in place to achieve your defined goals. Each of those that comes to mind is an ability you need to pull off your vision. In our current example, we may come up with Canadian, Australian, and U.S. sales experience, perhaps along with supporting expertise like knowledge of local regulations and competitors.

Now, consider how these skill sets can be distributed between different roles. Our Canadian firm, for instance, may decide that their Australian operation will require one person used to dealing with advertising agencies in that country, another with experience of the wholesale sector in Australia, and so forth. Drawing up a provisional organogram may help at this stage. A lot of businesses are hierarchical in organizational structure, others are flat, and some are circular. Work with whichever suits your team's culture and structure.

Now, you have a good idea of what kind of structure will be required to deliver your business vision. You don't need, as yet, to concern yourself too much with the practicalities and costs of filling each vacant position. You will need to create a rough plan to bring the structure to life in the next 3 years, though. Some of the roles you've just defined may not be filled fully until the third year, though it's always a good idea to reserve an initial period for onboarding and training.

To repeat an important point: we've created 3-year strategic goals toward your long-term vision. The structure and planned roles of your elite team are based on these, so always keep your long-term vision in mind when playing around with different staffing plans. As an example, you may know that you will need a general manager to completely take over your role in seven years. Currently, you don't have anyone in your team who's a great fit for that role. Your hiring decisions in the next three years should be influenced by this necessity. You may, for instance, hire a sales or operations manager who will be able to fill the general manager role when it's time.

Don't limit your thinking solely because of the present size of your organization. It's entirely reasonable for a small business or even solopreneur to pursue a scale-up plan that requires external hires, as long as these are a way to fulfill their vision. In this case, you may plan to share multiple roles among a small team rather than hiring separate people for each.

2. Establish One Primary Deliverable (PD) for Each Role

Once you have a list of the roles you'll need to fill, write down one primary deliverable, or performance metric, for each function. Make sure that is measurable, clear, concise, and concrete.

A good example is for the role of a sales manager: "Deliver yearly sales revenue target set by the organization". At the start of the year, senior management will decide on a concrete sales figure that's achievable but also somewhat ambitious. (You can see the SMART system rearing its head again here.) This statement is clear and concise and will have a number attached to it, so the sales manager can track their progress and be held accountable to ensure that their primary deliverable is attained.

An example of a vague primary deliverable for the same role would be "deliver high sales performance". It's hard enough to figure out what "high sales performance" even means, let alone when it's been achieved. You might think it obvious that you're referring to multiple six figures in revenue when, in your sales manager's last role, $50,000 may have been considered acceptable. These kinds of numbers can differ dramatically between industries and businesses, so assuming that everyone is on the same page can lead to massive confusion.

Each role typically has multiple responsibilities, but the primary deliverable is what they will eventually be held accountable to. By only having one primary deliverable, you emphasize their main priority and tell them where you want their focus to be. Sales managers' other tasks like managing and coaching the sales team, developing sales strategies, sales reporting, liaising with the marketing team, and ensuring strong customer relationships, are also important, of course. Defining a single primary deliverable, however, ensures that these will be done in support of the primary goal without subsuming it in a tidal wave of tasks that are all considered crucial.

3. Establish One Corresponding Primary Deliverable Number for the Primary Deliverable (PDN)

Have you ever seen job descriptions that run to two or three pages, with so many responsibilities listed that the unlucky employee doesn't even know where to begin? At least half the time, expecting somebody to give their full attention to everything means they won't be able to do anything.

This is why having only one primary deliverable number is so useful: it gives a sharp focus to each role in the organization. There is no ambiguity and your team immediately prioritizes the right deliverables because their performance is evaluated based on those. The sales manager in our example will still be aware of other performance indicators, such as those relating to customer service and retention, but sales revenue is always going to be in the forefront of their minds.

Ideally, each employee's primary deliverable number is agreed upon at the time of hiring. Such a target can also be set to evaluate the performance of a probationary colleague. There's no need to overcomplicate this provision:

Role: Sales Head

Primary Deliverable (PD): Deliver sales revenue targets set by the organization.

Primary Deliverable Number (PDN): Quarterly sales revenue target of $200,000.

Appropriate metrics and numbers are best decided on in collaboration with the person who will be held accountable to them. When it is done unilaterally, i.e. saying: "You'll achieve whatever I give you as a target", the team member in question will most likely lack buy-in and won't be committed to achieving an apparently arbitrary goal. Collaboratively established goals are much more effective as motivators and planning tools.

Primary deliverable numbers aren't always easy to establish at first. Finding a balance between the realistic and the aspirational is both an art and a science. I recommend starting with whatever figure makes sense based on your experience and refining these over time.

In your organizational structure, the time period for each PDN can be yearly or quarterly. (In this way, they can be used for strategic planning.) The person responsible for them can then break them down further into weekly or monthly targets.

Sales targets, for instance, will differ depending on how the organization and industry work and the frequency of reporting. The important thing is to make sure your accountability number makes sense on an intuitive level. A weekly target would be appropriate if you have regular weekly sales review meetings. If your service or product is too substantial and expensive to expect at least one sale per week, a quarterly target will be more meaningful.

Once the elite team design process is complete, your business team leadership organogram may look something like the following. Note that this is a simplified representation of how the senior leaders are organized. Depending on your company's size and structure, you may need additional departmental lines or leadership layers.

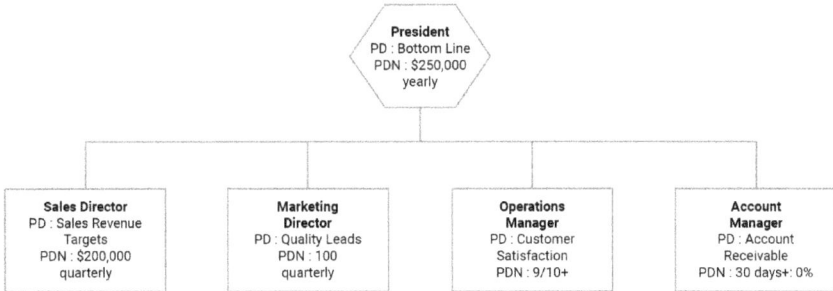

<Sample Accountability Structure>

The goal of this chart is accountability. There should be no ambiguity regarding its purpose and meaning. Anybody should be able to look at the diagram and see what everyone is responsible for and what target they're aiming to reach. This allows everyone to hold each other accountable, and just as importantly, to support one another effectively.

4. Skill Sets and Qualities

At this point, you have your elite team's structure mapped out in terms of roles, with an associated primary deliverable and primary deliverable number for each. It is time to identify the skills and traits needed in those roles at a more granular level. Earlier, when we looked at the skill sets needed to actualize your business vision, we did so from a bird's eye view. In this step, we are concerned with how things may play out at an operational level; we'll therefore take a "worm's eye" perspective and see what specific skills we need in each role in order for the business to run smoothly.

Earlier, we spoke of a company with a need for Australian, Canadian and U. S. sales expertise. At a macro, structural level, broad terms such as these are appropriate. It's now time to qualify what we really mean by "sales expertise". What skills and qualities does each position require in order to succeed in its primary deliverable? Examples of how to stipulate these can be found in any job advertisement. Depending on the role, these prerequisites may be framed as years of experience in the field, numbers of solid contacts already established, specific educational qualifications, and so on.

5. Establish a One-Page Role Description for Each Position in Your Elite Team

Bring all the information above together in a one-page document for each role. This gives you a blueprint for your team development plan, internal or otherwise. The template is also downloadable here (https:// sustainablelifedesign.com/ScaleYourSmallBusiness).

Role:

Primary Deliverable:

Primary Deliverable Number:

Responsibilities:

Skills:

Personal Qualities:

Probation:

Next Level Role-Position

6. Plan Out Your Elite Team

Once you have defined the full structure above, it's time to start thinking about building the team in terms of "how?" and "when?". As with all aspects of your business, the foundation for this important project is your business vision. Review your three-year strategic objectives and the Year 1 to 3 goals based on these before you begin to plan out your team development.

What talented individuals will you need in Year 1, Year 2, and Year 3 respectively? Regardless of whether you intend to grow your own employees who are already part of the organization or plan to bring the right individuals from outside, this takes time and requires patience. Done well, of course, this can be a highly rewarding process that brings you significantly closer to achieving your SCALE-UP dream. If this is done hastily or indifferently, the best outcome you can expect is a severe delay in achieving your vision.

Some of your current team members may be good candidates for more responsible and demanding roles as long as their skills in certain areas are upgraded. Others may require more extensive training and development before promotion becomes a possibility. You may need to hire new people. These kinds of issues should all be considered in the context of the structure you've created for the elite team you'll eventually have. Being mindful of the work you've already done and being the kind of leader who understands the capacities of your existing team will supply you with the information and timelines you need to construct your SCALE-UP elite team.

One of my clients, Kelly, is currently doing exactly this. She has recognized that she needs to secure a general manager in order to reach her 3-year strategic goal. Currently, all of her team members report to her, creating a communications bottleneck and restricting her ability to manage her time as she'd like. The first thing she and I discussed was whether one of her current managers would be a good candidate to step up and become general manager in the next few years. This is a priority; Kelly wants to dedicate more time to developing and scaling up her business. Unfortunately, she doesn't currently have anyone working for her who displays the personal qualities and talents a general manager requires. Her current leaders are all more like project managers: experts in their respective fields but lacking a perspective broad enough to appreciate all the functions and divisions needed to make a company work.

Having identified the gaps in her team, Kelly now knows that the next time she hires a manager, she should be looking for someone with the potential to become her general manager. Why not just hire someone with appropriate experience right away? At this point, the business is not financially ready to hire a full-time general manager, nor does the workload justify having one. Even if this weren't the case, though, there are some risks involved in bringing in a senior leader with no experience of her business or its culture, such as them possibly turning out to be a bad fit. Of course, opting for an outside hire is exactly what she would have been forced to do at some future point if she hadn't taken the time to plan her elite team in advance.

Now that she's armed with this knowledge, let's say her sales manager leaves. She understands that the best outcome will be to hire a new person who's not just good at sales, but who also has the qualities needed to take on all or part of the general manager role as well as the ambition to develop as an executive leader. Hiring is no longer just about filling the immediate role, but looking ahead several years so that future roles can be filled by promoting internally. This is not only cost-effective but, more importantly, a huge morale boost for the team.

You may remember how, in Rachel's vision, she needed to have a general manager ready to replace her and take over all responsibility for day-to-day operations when she steps away from her current, active role. This is a vision for seven years in the future, but knowing exactly what she's aiming for allows her to map out a path to her future team structure. In her vision, she wants to have her current studio manager step up into the general manager role a couple of years before the vision has been fully actualized. The new manager would be fully responsible for the current studio and assist Rachel with opening her second branch.

Rachel was confident that her current studio manager is a great fit to assume operational control of the business eventually. Over the next three years, this manager has the opportunity to grow into a leadership role, enjoying ever more autonomy but still having access to Rachel's occasional input. This is a classic win-win solution and a good example of smart leadership. The manager's need for professional development, her commitment to the business's success, as well as her personal aspirations all correspond very nicely with the needs of the business. Including the manager in the long-term plan to build Rachel's elite team is an additional motivator and garners high-level commitment.

Rachel and her manager discussed their future plans and how the latter might step into a responsible leadership role. Rachel signed the manager up for my one-to-one leadership coaching program so she could expand her existing skills in this area. Since then, RYP has already opened its second studio and Rachel's manager has been instrumental in the success of this process.

Assuming that your business and your staff are aligned, the possibility of professional growth and promotion is highly motivating and invigorating for the team. When there is a disconnect between their respective purposes and core values, you will see apathy and insecurity instead. The misaligned team members may feel threatened because they see the business growing in a direction where they don't see a role for themselves. This may be an opportunity for your organization to assess their suitability moving forward and update future staffing plans accordingly. If some people leave because their purpose and values conflict with those of the company, it's best to see it as an opportunity to usher more of the right people onto the bus and continue assembling your elite team.

In Rachel's case, her soon-to-be-general manager feels highly valued by the company and is even more committed to improving her skills and contributing to the success of the business. There are multiple wins:

- Business win – The manager's growth both as a leader and a person allows Rachel to focus on opening the second studio and pursuing other expansion plans.

- Rachel's win – Rachel can see her manager growing and feels confident in her ability to lead not just the first studio but guide the managers of subsequent studios. It's clear that she will take over daily business operations in seven years. This is important for Rachel's freedom.

- Manager's win – The manager feels valued and fulfilled at work because she is growing and developing. She is also cultivating and nurturing her team in turn, leading to wins for additional stakeholders.

Build Your Elite Team Based on Your Design

If you want to create a workforce worthy of your business vision and goals, you will have to develop the current team and/or hire new talents from outside. There are pros and cons to each option and neither way is inherently better than the other. Both approaches take time and sometimes present you with short-lived opportunities, though – it pays to have a plan in mind for constructing your elite team.

Developing your current team members, who are already familiar with the organization and embedded in the culture, can lead to better team cohesion, loyalty, and morale. It's usually cost-efficient, too, as bringing in outside hires can be expensive once you factor in all the costs associated with recruitment. However, the downside of this option is that it limits the talent pool at your disposal. Your plans for scaling up may call for a particular skill set, which would take a prohibitively long time to develop in existing staff. There is also your staff's goals and values to consider: sometimes, the biggest challenge to promoting from within can be resistance to change.

Hiring from external sources gives you immediate access to proven, specialized expertise. New hires often bring fresh perspectives to processes and problem-solving, too. The main downside to outside hires is that external talent acquisition can be more expensive, while onboarding and integration take time.

In practice, the best approach usually involves a combination of both strategies. You can develop current employees for roles that align with their interests and potential while also selectively hiring new talent to address specific gaps in the team's skill set. With every slot you fill on your planned elite team's structure diagram, you are getting a little closer to achieving your vision.

Develop Your Team from Within

Let's imagine that you currently have an employee who is committed to her work and has demonstrated leadership potential over the years. It has been evident in your various conversations that she wants to grow with your company. You can see that there is a great fit between this employee's personal aspiration to develop as a leader and the business's need to have someone who can take charge of a growing team.

She has also proven her leadership qualities over the years, although she has no direct experience leading people in a business context. It's time to establish a development plan to take her from where she is now to where she needs to be. How, then, can you support and empower this person to become a strong leader over the coming years?

I suggest creating a Personal Growth Program to aid the process. This idea has evolved over the years and proven to be effective with my clients.

Personal Development Program – Internal

Developing an employee is just not going to happen during the course of a single meeting. Rather, you'll have to commit to a series of conversations and coaching sessions between you as leader and each direct report who shows potential. I don't prescribe exactly how you conduct these or what outcomes to strive for, as I find it more empowering and enjoyable when the leaders bring their own personal styles into the process. There are some universal principles to follow, though. In particular, the topics of alignment and growth must be covered in personal development programs.

Alignment is a rather broad subject. Generally speaking, though, it is where we draw motivation and commitment from. Together, explore:

- Alignment between an employee and your business's vision and goals: Does this person play a role in the vision at their current skill level or perhaps with an upgrade? Do you see a place for them in your collective future?

- Alignment of the future aspirations of the employee and the organization: Do the employee's future aspirations line up with those of the business? Does your business belong in the employee's future?

Some aspects to cover during this conversation include the employee's cultural fit, planned career growth trajectory, interests, personal vision, etc. With their degree of alignment established, we then create a growth program to support your employee to get to their next level.

How should the team member develop in order to get to where they need to be in the coming months and years? How often do you need to meet with them to further their success? The template that I recommend (downloadable in the resource page) starts with the "Wheel of Life" exercise we used back in Chapter 3 during the personal visioning process. In the course of the personal development program, leaders and their reports may get engaged in all elements of the wheel. Others will prefer to focus exclusively on the "Work and Finance" segment. It all depends on the existing relationship, as both leaders and direct reports may feel different levels of connection with one another.

As a leader, you will touch on issues such as the financial goals they may have. How does their work support these goals? If a salesperson wants to save for a down payment on their first condo, the accomplishment of an annual sales target may be an important goal for them if it includes a substantial bonus. If they include developing as a leader in their work goals, this too may be a good fit if the business SCALE-UP vision aligns with their other objectives. The growth program may then place more emphasis on developing their leadership skills and qualities.

This approach allows you to go beyond a traditional performance review and help each team member to make significant steps towards their goals, personal and professional. Implementing a personal development program will naturally motivate your employees because their personal success is aligned with the success of the business. In my experience, this approach to stimulating employee growth is rewarding and fulfilling for the leaders too, not to mention effective at facilitating the success of the business vision and goals.

Hire the Right People in the Right Seats – External

Let's say your sales and accounting roles are currently outsourced. Your vision may be to bring these functions in-house in the future. You'll need to hire two people to do this. You've already, while designing your elite team, mapped out approximately when they will be hired based on your budget and growth trajectory.

Constructing an elite team, including the hiring process, should prioritize cultural fit based on your core values and core purpose. Finding the right people is crucial; otherwise, they will be neither happy nor effective and are bound to leave eventually. A secondary, yet still essential, concern is to establish skill fits based on the role documents you established in Step 5 above. The best way to ensure that both of these requirements are met is to complete an interview sheet for each new hire. Be clear about who you are looking for (a cultural fit) and what abilities they need to have (as spelled out in the role document), and use the interview sheet to take notes on these aspects. An interview sheet template (downloadable) is available on my website (https://sustainablelifedesign.com/ScaleYourSmallBusiness); your specific needs can easily be layered onto it.

Here is a quick overview of the hiring process for small businesses. Note that we are staying at the macro level here.

1. Advertise the job or network to screen the right people in and the wrong people out. A carefully phrased job ad helps you save time and energy throughout the process. The ad will include

information about the role, primary and supporting deliverables, the key skill sets and qualities, and your company's core purpose and core values.

2. Conduct phone interviews to create a shortlist – After selecting your top candidates, conduct a quick telephonic interview and ask each candidate the same set of questions. These will be simple interviews to establish the basics: you will go into more detail during the video or in-person meetings. This saves you time by screening out bad cultural fits that weren't obvious from the resume or CV alone.

3. Schedule in-person or video interviews – These interviews are an opportunity to establish if the candidate's purpose and values are aligned with those of the organization and the requirements of the role. The questions are prepared in advance and are the same for all applicants. It's a good idea to quiz them on scenarios that have arisen in your business, so you can see if each candidate will handle certain problems in a way that fits your culture and deliverables. This is also an opportunity to share your vision with candidates you determine are a good fit and hear their ideas. Are they excited or overwhelmed by your vision? I recommend assembling a panel of interviewers instead of using a single one, assuming that this is practically feasible. This will provide objectivity and diversity. We inherently bring our personal bias into all things we do, so having multiple perspectives is always beneficial.

4. Collect scores and have an open discussion – Discuss the candidates with the other interviewers. Evaluate each of their important skills and qualities using a standardized scoring system. Focus on those attributes that pertain to the advertised role and any future opportunities the applicants may be suited for. The goal is to select the candidate who is the best fit for both present needs and the future vision.

5. (Optional) Spend half a day with the finalists – When hiring for key leadership positions, you and your key leaders may need to spend several hours with the finalists so you can learn more about each other. Each hire is an investment of time and money,

and carries rewards and risks. We want to reduce the risks and maximize the rewards as much as possible.

6. Inform all the candidates whether they were selected or not – Each and every encounter with people is an opportunity to strengthen your brand. Informing all the interviewees either way, while often neglected, will show that you respect their time and effort.

7. Don't settle for less than you need – It sometimes happens that you work through the whole process before having to confront the fact that none of the applicants you interviewed were truly suitable. Try to resist the knee-jerk response of choosing the least mediocre: hiring a bad cultural fit or someone without the skills required by the role is often worse than leaving the position empty. Instead, start over, perhaps advertising on different platforms or in a broader region.

The key to successful external hiring is to use your elite team design as a blueprint. This will have been built upon your vision and three-year strategic goals, ensuring that your hiring policy isn't out of sync with other business initiatives. Also consider your long-term vision. For Kelly, who wanted to establish a general manager as part of her long-term vision, her immediate need may be hiring a sales manager (for example). During the hiring process, she may lean towards a person who will make a great sales manager for her business in the next few years, but more importantly has the potential to grow into a competent general manager in the longer term. This would give her organization room to grow and provide her with more options in the future. Being able to either promote a new General Manager from within, hire one from outside, or share the responsibilities with other employees will give her flexibility to accommodate factors like her business structure and budget.

Your Action:

Design and Build Your Elite Team – Identify the people and skills your business needs to achieve your vision.

Creating a winning team doesn't happen by accident. If an elite team is needed to make your vision a reality, you have to start by imagining it as it will be in the future when your three-year goals have been accomplished. Don't use your current team as a starting point; instead, create an ideal structure with defined roles, including primary deliverables and primary deliverable numbers for each. Then, over the next few years, strike a balance between developing your existing employees and making suitable outside hires.

1. Design your elite team structure to fulfill your three-year strategic goals based on your vision.

2. Define the primary deliverable and the corresponding number for each role.

3. Sketch out a development plan to make the elite team structure a reality.

4. Establish regular one-on-one meetings with your direct reports to discuss their professional development, if you haven't yet.

5. Create a "personal growth program" for each promising employee.

PART III

BRING YOUR VISION TO LIFE: YOUR SYSTEM TO ACTUALIZE YOUR VISION AND GOALS

"Focus and simplicity… once you get there, you can move mountains."

– Steve Jobs

Chapter 12: Creating Unity – Ensuring You and Your Team Focus in One Singular Direction

Chapter 13: Establishing Processes of Success – Setting Up Accountability Mechanisms to Accomplish Your Goals and Vision Through Tools, Reports, and Meetings

Thus far in this book, you have developed into a strong and confident rower (Part I: Self Leadership) and built a powerful boat with a talented crew to take you to your dream destination (Part II: Solid Business Foundation). Everyone on the boat knows where they are heading and more importantly, is psyched about it.

Now, it's time to insulate the success of your vision against challenges, small and large, that you will inevitably have to face. Any number of obstacles can push you off course along the journey. At this time, let's ensure that you have a system in place that will help you stay on course so that you can actualize your vision and your team's ambitions.

Simply having a plan or goal doesn't guarantee success – New Year's resolutions are the perfect example of this fact. Goals become sources of frustration rather than fulfillment when we fall short. How do we ensure success regardless of the setbacks we're bound to encounter along the way?

As we've discussed at length, an inspiring vision is essential to business success. When you and your team are genuinely inspired by your vision, you are all more likely to remain motivated, persevere through difficulties, and adapt your plans when necessary. Inspiration fuels our determination and helps us to maintain a positive mindset throughout the journey.

Even then, we are frequently and amply challenged by various factors. Like our New Year's resolutions, a vision that's not supported by specific goals and a system to achieve them may still be inspiring: we want to lose weight so that we feel healthier and more attractive, we want to start saving money to achieve financial freedom, or finally start scaling up our business to fulfill our life dreams. Yet, those apparently inspirational resolutions stubbornly fail to materialize.

This is largely because we possess some very human tendencies we inherited from our evolutionary history. Conserving energy. Path of least resistance. Laziness. Call it what you will, but we all tend to "take it easy" if we can and just hope for the best. Unfortunately, in business, that strategy doesn't work. Some of the most common reasons for failing to meet our business goals are:

- Now over later – The demands of the present often take precedence over our vision because we are busy reacting to daily events. There is a never-ending deluge of customer requests, complaints, and new needs due to changes in our external environment.

- Favouring the path of least residence – One of the most common hurdles to success is the tendency to put off important tasks in favour of more immediate, easier, or more pleasurable activities. These tasks divert valuable time and attention that could be devoted to working toward our goals.

- Lack of focus – The abundance of information and constant connectivity we have at our fingertips is as much of a curse as it is a blessing. It is easy to become distracted by social media, emails, notifications, new tools, and other external stimuli. This can lead to a loss of focus and a diminished ability to complete the tasks necessary to achieve our goals.

- Too many priorities, hence no real priority – Priorities and interests abound. New opportunities, unexpected circumstances, or setbacks all compete for our time and energy. Our original objectives get lost in all the background noise.

- As a result, we become a servant instead of the master of our most valuable resource: time. Balancing the numerous responsibilities and commitments that crowd our daily lives can make it challenging to pursue our goals effectively. We get overwhelmed by to-do lists and disempowered by constant distractions.

Overcoming these challenges requires an actualization system to support your efforts to stay on track. The framework for achieving your ambitions focuses on your vision, prioritizes your SMART goals, and works toward your pre-established milestones.

This actualization system is the business equivalent of your personal productivity routine. It unites you and your team, directs your attention to the business vision, and ensures that there are processes in place to communicate collective and individual progress regularly and transparently. Your actualization system will also hold you and your entire team accountable to your milestones and celebrate the progress you make.

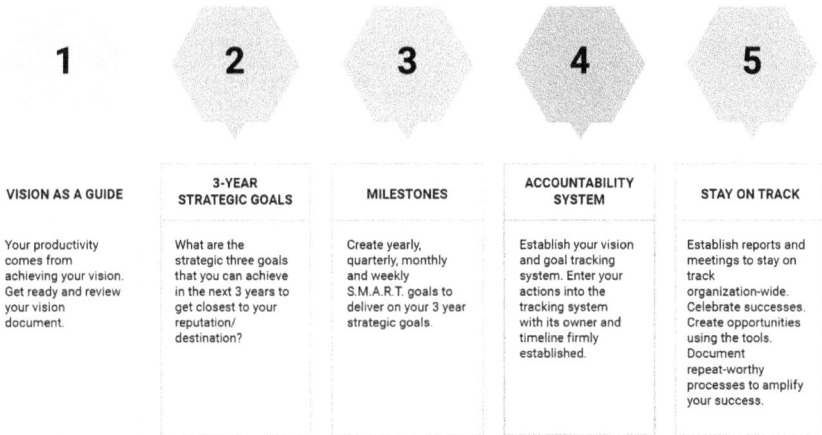

1	**2**	**3**	**4**	**5**
VISION AS A GUIDE	3-YEAR STRATEGIC GOALS	MILESTONES	ACCOUNTABILITY SYSTEM	STAY ON TRACK
Your productivity comes from achieving your vision. Get ready and review your vision document.	What are the strategic three goals that you can achieve in the next 3 years to get closest to your reputation/destination?	Create yearly, quarterly, monthly and weekly S.M.A.R.T. goals to deliver on your 3 year strategic goals.	Establish your vision and goal tracking system. Enter your actions into the tracking system with its owner and timeline firmly established.	Establish reports and meetings to stay on track organization-wide. Celebrate successes. Create opportunities using the tools. Document repeat-worthy processes to amplify your success.

<The Process of Actualization>

This graphic shows the process needed to actualize your vision. In prior chapters, we established (1) your vision and (2) the three-year SMART goals that mark the path toward that vision. In Part III, we will break them down into (3) time-bound actions, (4) establish ownership for each of these actions, and (5) install processes of success in our business that ensure that our team is unified and accountable.

We are in the last mile of the book. The finish line is very near, so let's stay focused on getting there.

CHAPTER 12

CREATING UNITY – ENSURING YOU AND YOUR TEAM FOCUS IN ONE SINGULAR DIRECTION

"We are only as strong as we are united, as weak as we are divided."

– J.K. Rowling, British author and philanthropist

Imagine a rowing team, each crew member pulling in unison towards the finish line. The power generated by their synchronized effort propels the boat forward with remarkable speed and efficiency. Now, imagine what would happen if the members of rowing team were all rowing in slightly different directions – toward where each rower believed the finish line lay. They are all operating with the best of intentions, but their disunity is steering the collective effort off course. Even if they all want to head in the same general direction but are rowing at slightly divergent angles or to different rhythms, they will not be as efficient as a team that is completely synchronized.

Similarly, in your business, when your team joins forces and works together in harmony, unity can take your company to new levels. Your organization becomes greater than the sum of all its parts as your team collaborates, motivates one another, and joins their strengths toward the actualization of your ambitious vision. This energy breeds resilience and confidence in your collective capabilities. Obstacles, no matter how seemingly insurmountable, are no match for a unified effort. We don't have to look far for examples of incredible achievements by teams. Think about the history of any field; you will marvel at what people have achieved when working together.

Just like the rowing team reaches their destination more quickly when pulling in unison, businesses go further and faster when their teams pool their efforts in one synchronized effort. They become an unstoppable force in the face of whatever challenges lie ahead. Businesses' productivity, profitability, and prosperity all arise from unity.

With all that being said, most organizations still find it incredibly difficult to consistently achieve this ideal. Even with everyone nominally working towards a shared vision, slightly differing intentions on the part of various team members can result in a loss of efficiency. This is quite normal; some disunity is to be expected, but this doesn't mean we shouldn't try to minimize it. The key is to continuously put agreed-upon processes in place to actualize your vision. This significantly increases the chances of maintaining unity of purpose and action. The result, naturally, is timely progress toward the business vision and, more than incidentally, individual team members' goals.

Accordingly, in this chapter we'll explore the concept of unity in three parts. The first concerns achieving unity of vision, or in other words having one finish line to inspire your team. The second covers the processes needed to keep everyone on the prearranged course. Lastly, we'll talk about remaining united through a shared commitment to being accountable.

United Behind a Shared Vision

The first step to working in concert is to make sure your business vision is being embraced by the whole team. A necessary prerequisite for this is that this vision creates multiple wins for everyone involved. In other words, the vision should be conducive to each and every individual's success as well as collective progress.

The best way of achieving this is to involve employees in the creation of your business vision, as described in detail in Part II of this book. The gold standard for the visioning process is for all team members (and even external partners) to have a stake in the result.

In practical terms, it's not always possible to allow your whole team to provide thorough input at every stage of defining your vision. Regardless, once your vision statement, together with the business core strengths on which it rests and the objectives which follow from it, are established, it is imperative that you share it diligently with everyone. At this point, you have a comprehensive yet concise foundation on which you can build a unified team. Letting it go to waste due to a lack of communication would be a real shame.

You may choose to share the business vision through an all-hands meeting, ideally one that's regularly scheduled and attended by everyone. Explain your inspiring vision to the team and ensure that you all have a conversation instead of delivering a lecture. Allow them to give input into the setting of goals and scheduling of actions. What thoughts do they have about the vision? In what ways can they contribute to making it a reality? Does anything in the vision need to evolve based on their experiences and expertise? Even a one-person operation may seek advice from other stakeholders like a life partner, investors, or whoever is closely involved with the business (or could potentially support its success in some way).

A company-wide conversation should help sort out any dissonance and misalignment between your vision and the team that's expected to bring it to fruition. If there is a disconnect between the top leader's aspirations for the company and the wants and needs of individuals at different levels of the business, the vision will fail to create the hoped-for unity. A vision drafted by management which junior-level employees cannot relate to will result in apathy instead. A demotivated, divided team is highly unlikely to row in unison or toward the same finish line. Be prepared to let your vision and goals evolve based on your team's feedback. Not only you will generate greater buy-in, you will also find that their viewpoints provide valuable perspectives.

The visioning process, if well executed and shared with the right people (meaning a strong tribe that shares the same purpose and core values) should energize the whole team. Once the vision, three-year strategic plan, and goals for Years 1 to 3 are actively embraced by the entire group, shorter-term and more discrete goals and actions can be worked out at the departmental or individual level, depending on the size and structure of the company.

This is a tall order, a big ask. I don't mean to imply that doing all of this is easy or something that can be accomplished in a week. However, the benefits to your business and its culture are immense. Like with all great achievements, the rewards totally justify the significant amount of work you'll need to do to attain unity in your business.

At this stage, every team member should find their alignment with the business vision. There are some members who may not see a future with your company; that is good because you have the opportunity to replace them with new teammates who are better aligned with your vision, core values, and growth plan. You need to select your crew carefully. Personal Growth Programs are a valuable tool for building your elite team, as is implementing processes to track each team's performance.

United Behind Agreed-Upon Processes

Once you have a shared vision, it is important that your vision can be discerned in every facet of your business life. Your vision is the thought and feeling that underpins everything your business does. It should be visible everywhere your brand is present, online and offline, it should be an active part of the team's daily lives, and it should inform the processes they adhere to at work.

Tasks orientated at achieving the business vision need to be baked into daily, weekly, and long-term processes so that the vision comes alive in your operations. This way, your vision is translated from an abstract concept to practical action. Just as importantly, your vision will be front and centre in all your business operations. Processes, meetings, and reporting standards will all emphasize objectives related to your business vision. Little time and effort will be wasted on ancillary goals that aren't directly linked to your business purpose. Ways to accomplish this while avoiding various pitfalls are discussed in more detail in the next chapter, Establishing Processes of Success.

Without this focus on the business vision running through all your business processes, you are leaving it up to individuals to incorporate the vision into their work. This presents an inherent risk of everyone rowing in a slightly different direction or to an offbeat rhythm.

You may well have experienced this phenomenon yourself: you and some colleagues have a meeting and leave in total agreement, yet later you discover that every one of you had a somewhat different understanding of what was decided. This happens because we all have unique expectations, perceptions, and assumptions. By spelling out, as clearly, concisely, and concretely as possible, what needs to be done to pursue your vision, you ensure that everyone is truly on the same page.

In any collective endeavour, if we want to achieve great things, we need to make certain that everyone's goals are truly the same and not just similar. The alternative means a lot of wasted energy and reinventing the wheel several times. If your team is inspired but also slightly confused by the way you communicated your vision, your rowers will be rowing as hard as they can but in different directions. Ironically, in this case, they won't arrive at the destination as quickly as they could despite their commitment and good intentions. This is only one way in which a lack of unity in processes can leave your team feeling utterly frustrated.

In order to reinforce a universal understanding of what the vision means on a practical level, we create milestones and specify everyone's role in the vision. Defined, documented business processes exist to ensure that your team stays committed to the vision and continues to make progress toward it. Even people with the best intentions and highest levels of motivation can drift from the planned course (or drop their oars, as it were) when they face challenges. Processes of success, as described in the next chapter, are put in place to ensure that the vision is regularly communicated and the entire team is held accountable for their progress towards the business's goals.

United Behind Accountability

When you outline each team member's role and contribution to the business vision and goals, you automatically establish certain responsibilities for them. When everybody is committed to these responsibilities, they all start out with the right mindset – but this, by itself, is not enough.

Allow me to reiterate a previous point: intention doesn't always equal action. Signing up for our part in an ambitious plan complete with SMART goals gives most of us a warm, fuzzy feeling. This, unfortunately, constitutes a psychological trap, namely that of falsely equating intent and achievement. If you want your team to actually move the needle, you need to hold them accountable and, if necessary, ask them to correct their course.

Promoting your vision in a way that gets people excited is a good beginning but gives no guarantee for the actualization of your business vision. Accountability, for everyone including leaders, is what we need to keep the boat moving in the right direction with all the rowers pulling in sync. Prioritize accountability over harmony, if necessary, and hold everyone accountable to the vision and processes they agreed to.

Your Action:

Ensure Unity to Create Effortless Wins – Get everybody on the same page as to what your vision means and how it will be achieved.

The sweeping concept of "unity" is somewhat difficult to define, but it (or its absence) is easy to spot in a company's operations. Like culture, it cannot simply be imposed on an organization, though a leader can certainly take steps to foster it. Some important aspects of this are clearly communicating the vision, instituting appropriate processes, and maintaining accountability across the board.

1. Plan and share your vision and 3-year strategic plan at your next general team meeting. How can you make it inspiring and engaging? How can you elicit the most participation from everyone?

2. Determine how you will track your progress. Some options are a spreadsheet hosted on the company intranet, various online tools, and regular strategy review meetings.

CHAPTER 13

ESTABLISHING PROCESSES OF SUCCESS – SETTING UP ACCOUNTABILITY MECHANISMS TO ACCOMPLISH YOUR GOALS AND VISION THROUGH TOOLS, REPORTS, AND MEETINGS

"Success is a process. Not an event."

– Gary Halbert, eminent copywriter

In the previous chapter, we discussed the importance of unity. With this unity established around an unwavering focus on the business vision, it's time to create our processes for success. What good is our vision if it's not materialized? Jim Carrey might have written a 10-million-dollar cheque for himself and just dreamt on. That's hardly a recipe for achievement. So many of us daydream about a future in which we don't need to work for money. Financial freedom can seem like such an enormous and intangible goal considering our current reality. Your dream lifestyle seems like nothing more than a dream – unless you have a system and plan to actualize it.

What makes some people achieve their dreams? Why do so many of us not? Some of the reasons were offered in earlier chapters, along with solutions. One thing that can set you on the road to success, for instance, is having a clear vision. Saying "I want to be rich one day" is just too vague to make a concrete plan around. "I want my business to prosper one day" doesn't give us the specifics we need to create a roadmap.

As a starting point, we created our ambitious vision, with definite goals and a date on which we want to achieve them. Because we don't want to sacrifice our present happiness to get to the finish line more quickly, perhaps only to realize that we're not fulfilled when we arrive, we established our vision based on our "why?" – what it is that fulfills us?"

A lot of us have an ambitious vision, yet it remains forever a dream. The challenge may be that we don't know where to start. We have the desire to scale our businesses but wonder: "How can I possibly get from here to there?"

During my corporate career as leader of a global sales and marketing team, I was often asked how I could remain so calm and unstressed even when major challenges or pressing issues were bearing down on us. I used to reply: "One thing at a time." The sense of being overwhelmed comes from the cumulative size of all our obstacles. If we break these obstacles to our success into bite-size tasks and projects, we suddenly have something much more manageable to work on. That's exactly what I envisioned the SCALE UP system to be. Seen as a whole, scaling up a small business seems like an enormous and perhaps impossible challenge. Once it's systematically broken down according to the SCALE-UP framework, though, it can be dealt with one frame at a time.

As part of the method, we broke your vision down into three-year strategic goals, then used these as a basis for more granular yearly goals. In this chapter, you will translate these into even more specific, action-orientated tasks to be scheduled in your and your team's calendars. One day and one week at a time, you get closer to your finish line.

At this stage, you should have selected a tool to track your goals and actions toward your vision. Should that be a shared spreadsheet or an online platform? Whichever you choose, you will understand the need for strong buy-in from your team.

Another important process you need to have in place is a scheduling tool. Again, whatever works for you and your team for programming your vision-driven activities is fine, but choosing some kind of platform for this is essential. Personally, I find MS Outlook to be highly effective. It has served me and countless others whom I've worked with well over the years and it's very inexpensive. If your team already uses a shared calendar, that's a perfect foundation to build on as long as it supports functions like recurring appointments.

There is an important rationale behind establishing these tools to aid us in overcoming our innate human afflictions and limitations: "Know thyself," as the Ancient Greeks said. When we know that we will encounter obstacles, both internal and external, we can plan ahead and find ways to remove as many of them as possible. Let me explain how scheduling can help overcome two such human limitations:

Working memory limitation: The concept of working memory limitations is a well-established idea in cognitive psychology and neuroscience. We can only hold and process a finite amount of information in our heads at any given time. This is called working memory; our ability to hold temporary information. A computer's RAM offers a close parallel. As we near this limit, we find it increasingly difficult to remember details and prioritize multiple tasks and goals simultaneously.

Most people are aware of this, even if we don't know the scientific term. Anecdotally, we sometimes talk about cramming so much into our heads that things start to fall out. I expect that most business owners know from experience that they're extra stressed when there is a lot on their minds. That is the reason that many current and aspiring entrepreneurs already use to-do lists. This kind of daily agenda offers one way of remembering all our most important tasks.

This is certainly helpful, but not perfect. What the to-do list cannot help you with is prioritizing tasks: unfortunately, it puts every item at an equal level, encouraging you to try to do everything all at once. If it gets too long, a to-do list can become a stressor rather than a productivity hack. Scheduling, on the other hand, is an effective way to give the the proper emphasis to activities related to your SMART goals. It is inherently prioritized and time-bound.

Present bias: There is a second affliction that all human beings struggle with, referred to as "present bias" by psychologists. It is in our nature to prioritize immediate gratification over long-term rewards. The tasks right in front of us or actions that provide an immediate payoff are easier to put first because progress is obvious and immediate. Our sense of instant achievement is literally reflected in our brain chemistry, while long-term progress provides only a more abstract and intellectual pleasure. It is naturally difficult for us to allocate time and effort to work on goals that will only be realized in the distant future.

However, by breaking big goals down into smaller ones and making them time-bound, we are actually making progress towards the important stuff on a daily and weekly basis, one step at a time. For example, your financial freedom vision was first broken down into three-year goals, then dissected all the way down to weekly and daily objectives. You may, for instance, decide that you need to spend this week doing research on how other people achieved their dreams. You schedule half an hour each morning. When you wake up, this appointment with yourself is already in your calendar, prompting you to get started.

The processes of success we'll explore in this chapter are practical tools to ensure that our ambitious vision is actualized systematically and not just "when we get around to it". They produce timely work and bring your vision into today taking advantage of your natural "present bias" to help you achieve our vision. Because the overall objectives are broken down into daily and weekly activities and scheduled in our team's calendar, regular progress is assured. We're no longer wrestling with an intangible dream, but walking a defined path to achieving our vision.

These processes have two main intentions behind them: (1) actualizing your vision and (2) optimizing operations, hence bringing about productivity and profitability. It will be helpful to keep these motives in mind as you examine the specifics of the processes of success and consider how they can be adapted to the needs of your organization.

The Process of Actualization

Let's review and, if necessary, make last-minute tweaks to the important elements that you've worked hard to establish so far. We'll need to be absolutely clear on these so we can be confident in the plan we're going to present to our team.

1. Review and Revise Your Three-Year Strategic and Yearly Goals

Having established your long-term vision (for five to ten years into the future), we created three-year goals toward this finish line. These goals are strategic in nature and will ensure that you are building toward the vision. Achieving each represents a giant step in the direction of your ideal life.

Rachel from our earlier examples had her strategic goals established toward her long-term vision: (1) to have developed a reliable and competent leader to take over the daily operations of the first studio from her, and (2) to have built a profitable second studio. These two accomplishments will allow her to expand to four studios, thus achieving a major part of her seven-year vision. Once she's also established strong leadership in each of the additional three branches, she will have made her dream lifestyle a reality. These three-year strategic goals were then refactored into Year 1, 2, and 3 goals. Just like achieving her three-year goals brings her closer to her seven-year vision, these intermediate goals are stepping stones toward being where she wants to be in three years.

2. Set Smaller Milestones and Actions Toward Your Year 1 Goals

Have your Year 1 goals in front of you. Now, we will be translating these into smaller accomplishments and actions. Your yearly goals will become quarterly milestones, your quarterly milestones will be broken down into monthly goals, and your monthly goals will be turned into weekly activities and added to your schedule.

Let's take an example of developing promising leaders because, for many businesses, this is often a strategic part of their scale-up plans. It's a fact that business owners generally cannot expand without having a solid person or team to take charge of their daily operations. Sometimes, this is because scaling up requires more people; naturally, we need strong leadership to support a larger team. In another sense, trying to manage too many people directly leads to a loss of effectiveness in communication and oversight. Looking forward, next-level leadership is also essential if a business owner wants to spend less time on day-to-day operations, either to pursue other business development initiatives or engage in non-commercial activities directed at their personal fulfillment.

If your first-year goal is to secure a general manager, you can either promote from within, strengthen the leadership skills of someone who's already part of your team, or hire in a new manager. For the purposes of this exercise, let's say you think the most effective option is to go for an external hire. At present, you may not have anyone suitable inside the organization nor time to develop them. What should your Q1 goal be in order to have established new leadership by the end of Q4? It may look like this:

By the end of:

Quarter 1: We have compiled a list of top candidates.

Quarter 2: We have hired a general manager (and kept the runner-up candidate on file as a contingency plan) and completed their induction program.

Quarter 3: The new general manager has been with us through a full quarter cycle and is well-integrated into the team. The manager has received a strong endorsement from 95% of their direct reports.

Quarter 4: The general manager is the go-to person for the current team for support on daily operations.

Now, let's break these goals down into even smaller units. In order to have a list of top candidates by the end of Quarter 1, what must you accomplish in the next few days and weeks? The actions you come up with in this step are now small and actionable enough to be scheduled in your calendar.

Another very common goal is to achieve and maintain a certain sales revenue number. Based on your three-year strategic goals and yearly plans, you set a sales goal of one million dollars for Year 1. That figure needs to be broken down into smaller targets informed by past performance. Our past is a good predictor of our future actions and achievements, although these don't have to be determined by what has happened before. Some crucial information in this process is seasonal variations and our historical growth pattern.

Seasonal variations: Some months in our business may normally yield higher sales than others. Retailers and gyms may see 50% of their revenue in December and January respectively. These fluctuations will need to be reflected in your projections; growth goals have to be grounded in reality and take external factors into account.

Historical growth pattern: What can you learn from your growth in the past years? Let's say you have been growing by 10% year-on-year and your ambitious vision challenges you to achieve 20% in the next twelve months. What can you do to make that happen? Instead of adjusting your planned growth downwards, you should consider ways to improve your productivity. If we were to go with the status quo, we wouldn't have created our ambitious vision and we would just stay with the same old, same old, right?

The subject of forecasting and projecting sales numbers is too expansive a topic to discuss in full here. For now, let's focus on the process of setting quarterly goals and milestones.

Break your annual targets into quarterly goals, then monthly figures. Take seasonal aspects into account, but don't lose sight of achieving your yearly goals. If booking 1 million dollars by the end of the year is your goal and February is usually a slow month, adjust your monthly targets accordingly.

Now, recast these monthly figures as numbers to achieve each week. Ideally, this will be a collaborative process involving the sales associates and their leader. Done with frankness and respect, this can be an inspiring experience for all concerned. Too often, though, the procedure amounts to the boss dictating a target to their sales reps and hanging some incentives on it. We humans are not just money-driven machines. As touched on in Chapter 10, on leadership, and the previous chapter on creating unity, people are far more complex in their motives and have a broader idea of their self-interest. When your team members are empowered and invited to discuss important issues as equals, their commitment and focus on the business vision grow to match your own.

Your quarterly goals may look like this:

Quarter 1: $200,000
Quarter 2: $250,000
Quarter 3: $250,000
Quarter 4: $300,000

Now let's break this down into monthly targets. It may look like as follows:

Month 1: $70,000
Month 2: $60,000
Month 3: $70,000
etc.

Your monthly goals will then need to become weekly goals.

Week 1: $20,000
Week 2: $20,000
Week 3: $17,000
Week 4: $13,000

3. Schedule the Actions in Your Team's Calendar, Collectively and Individually, Then Enter the Goals and Actions in Your Preferred Tracking Platform

Let's say you have networking and advertisement as important Q1 actions. You will have broken these down into events to attend, meetings to have, campaigns to prepare, and so forth. Schedule these actions into your calendar, or one shared with your team if appropriate.

As for the quarterly sales revenue targets, you will already have split these all the way down to weekly goals. Once these goals are set, they are part of your accountability platform and tracked on a weekly basis. Whether you evaluate and celebrate weekly progress during regular meetings, display them on a poster in some prominent location, or use an online tracking platform will depend on the nature of your organization.

Go through all of your strategic and yearly goals and break them down into actions as described above. This may be easier with quantifiable targets like sales numbers, but less tangible forms of progress, like enhancing your company's online visibility, can also be separated into more easily achievable goals and translated into daily, weekly, and monthly actions to take.

4. Establish an Owner for Each Action or Project

Ensure that each task and project has a designated owner. This owner is responsible for getting the task completed and, just as importantly, is supplied with the resources and authority needed to take the necessary steps. Without an owner established, one of two things can happen. Either no one steps up to drive the job to completion, or those who have a stronger sense of duty and responsibility overcommit themselves. Neither of these is ideal, so it is best to pre-determine which individuals will be accountable for what. Then include their names in team calendar tasks and the platform you chose to track your goals. Aside from ensuring accountability, this lets everybody know who to talk to when their work either converges with or may potentially hinder other tasks.

One propensity I often notice in my clients is their bias toward trying to do everything all on their own. If you already have a team, consider assigning ownership of projects as an opportunity to empower and enable them within the limits of their capability. Assigning someone a task they are not prepared for is obviously futile, but it's also a mistake to underestimate what skills and talents your team possesses. You may be surprised at the rewards letting go of the reins a little bit can yield: people often possess capabilities their usual role doesn't allow them to display or develop. When people are empowered and supported, they tend to thrive. My blog contains several examples and some guidance on making this happen.

This does not necessarily mean that they'll be able to perform the assigned task without some development and guidance from you. Always remember that our team can do a great deal once they are trusted and given the right tools i.e., training, advice, and/or other resources. If any areas for improvement are identified during this process and you've decided to become a CGO (Chief Growth Officer), these can be addressed in each employee's personal growth program.

5. Review the Progress as a Team – Ongoingly!

Defined goals, be they numbers or qualitative outcomes, provide us with milestones. They tell us whether we are on track toward our business vision. It's no use only finding out in ten years' time (or whatever horizon you've chosen) whether we've succeeded or failed; we need an indication of whether or not we need to correct our course in the coming weeks and months.

If, for instance, your sales numbers are higher than predicted by your past performance, ask yourself what has changed for that improvement to be possible. How can you take better advantage of things going your way? You may have added two more people to your sales team, meaning your business has increased the number of accounts it can actively manage. You may have dropped a resource-intensive or unprofitable service or product, allowing your team to spend more time on your profitable verticals. In either case, doing more of the same may make sense, or it may be time to explore a new direction. Just make sure your performance metrics, and certainly the primary deliverable numbers we discussed in Chapter 11 with regards to building an elite team, are chosen according to strong rationales. If your product is designed to last for several years, for instance, customer retention is less of a priority.

Conversely, what if the achieved numbers are lower than the targets? Whether internal or external, the challenges you identify by examining the causes of underperformance will guide your future direction. What strategies will you implement, what opportunities will you pursue? When you design your goal framework around a long-term business vision and break it down into smaller goals and actions, it becomes easier to distinguish weekly blips from more general trends. However, you have to evaluate your progress on a weekly basis to maintain your strategic objectivity.

Each review like this is likely to generate additional actions, whether remedial or opportunistic. Add them onto your tracking platform and schedule them into your calendar. This very process of constant review and adjustment is a major driver of your success. When you do this conscientiously, you don't have to start every workday by reflecting on the business vision: you only need to pay attention to the scheduled tasks.

6. Resolve Underperformance as Soon as It Occurs

I've mentioned the idea of "conversations worth having" before, in Chapter 10 on leadership. As we've established, these do not need to be confrontational or unkind. Instead, they should be focused on generating multiple wins. Once you embrace this mindset, having a dialogue about missed weekly, monthly or quarterly targets becomes much more invigorating. It's also true that any conversation worth having is worth having sooner rather than later. These are truly opportunities to foster growth. Underperforming individuals often need nothing more than a little support to shine.

One of my clients was frustrated that he and his team weren't completing their vision-orientated tasks on schedule. If this happens to you (and it's quite a common occurrence), it's a good idea to invite the team or an individual (if it is a specific person in your organization) to a brainstorming session around the challenges that underlie their failure to meet defined, agreed-upon targets.

The intention isn't to lay blame or grumble about the challenges you're facing, but to find solutions (or as I like to call them, "opportunities") moving forward. Generally, I suggest approaching these issues with the question: "What worked in the past in a similar situation?" Without addressing the issue, you will most likely see continued underperformance, not only by the particular colleague (and this can be you by the way) but in the rest of the team. The last thing you want to do is signal that a failure to meet goals, poor-quality work, or a lack of focus on the business vision is something that will be excused.

You will already have implemented a platform that allows sharing the team's calendar as well as a tracking tool to record your collective and individual actions and progress. These are extremely valuable tools for any business and especially an organization trying to scale up. They're not the only ones you need, though. The following two tools support continuous improvement and accountability across all levels of your organization.

Reports that Promote Accountability

Structured reports are the most straightforward way to communicate progress and ensure accountability with respect to your vision and goals. They show numbers and accomplishments in black and white so everyone can see where headway is being made and where changes may be necessary. The kind of reports each leader requires will depend on the type of business.

You don't need to restrict these to bare-bones data, though. Reports that include narratives give context to the numbers. This allows the owner of a task, process, or project to give their views on why the team underperformed or overperformed. Knowing what happened is of obvious value when you're tracking your progress toward your business vision. Mere metrics, however, do not provide an actionable explanation of what caused delays or other unexpected outcomes.

Relevant reports should always be reviewed before meetings by everyone participating so that time can be used efficiently. We will get to the essentials of structuring meetings that effectively address challenges and opportunities in the next section. For now, though, let's just point out that all participants showing up prepared is far superior to them just showing up. How many times have you seen colleagues frantically rifling through spreadsheets trying to make sense of the discussion instead of playing a meaningful part? One way to encourage this desired behaviour is to request questions in advance of the meeting.

Track Your Vision, Goals and Actions on the Platform as a Unified Team

The platform used for your performance reporting and tracking should be visible and accessible to everyone. That way, the organization is united behind the agreed-upon process. Everyone will know what is expected of them and understand what their colleagues may be busy with. Having a master document as well as supporting departmental versions is often necessary for businesses with multiple departments (though it's not a bad idea to allow all employees to be able to view the master document). Here is an example of how a three-year strategic goal can be broken down into yearly goals and yearly departmental goals:

3-YEAR STRATEGIC GOALS					
	Specific	Due by	Owned by	Notes on the progress	Date completed
1	The second product line to achieve sales of $250,000	Year 3	Marketing, Sales & Operations		
2					
3					
4					
5					

Year 1 - GOALS		YEARLY GOALS			
	Specific	Due by	Owned by	Notes on the progress	Date completed
1	The second product line to be determined	20-Mar	Marketing Head		
2	Marketing communication complete for the 2nd product	20-Apr	Marketing Head		
3	Sales team to connect with the existing clients	31-May	Sales Head		
4	Operations team to get ready for the delivery	31-May	Operations Head		
5					

<Sample Tracking System for the Organization>

Year 1 - Goal 1	Actions - Marketing team	Due by	Owned by	Notes on the progress	Date completed
a	Market research - size of the market for second product	31-Jan	John		
b	Market research - competition VS our market share possibility	31-Jan	Lisa		
c	Market research - focus group planning	14-Feb	Lisa		
d					
e					

<Sample Tracking System for a Department>

The two most important columns here are "due by" and "owned by." Together, those two columns create accountability.

Track Departmental Performance

Departmental reports are intended to track the performance of both teams and individuals. The team's monthly or weekly performance targets are broken down into individual targets based on each team member's experience and ability.

The sales department's revenue target of $200,000 per quarter may be broken down like in the example below:

	Quarter 1 Goals	Weekly Goals	1-Jan	8-Jan	15-Jan	22-Jan	29-Jan	5-Feb	...
Sales rep 1	$ 75,000	$ 5,800							
Sales rep 2	$ 75,000	$ 5,800							
Sales rep 3	$ 25,000	$ 1,900							
Sales rep 4	$ 25,000	$ 1,900							
Sales Total	$ 200,000	$ 15,400							

<Sample Individual Goals>

Weekly reporting is then used to track progress toward the goal and to generate useful data by analyzing performance. Both underperformance and overperformance should be analyzed because either can inform us about the road ahead. As mentioned, it is important to address challenges as soon as they arise. Even more importantly, we should strive to find ways of repeating success. This review process allows you to harness collective learning to further elevate the team. In the example above, there is probably a reason why the senior sales reps generate three times the revenue of their less experienced counterparts. Chances are that they'll be happy to teach their methods to their colleagues.

Let's say, using the above example, that your team only achieved $12,000 instead of the hoped-for $15,400 in sales for the week. Creating a forum where the sales team can discuss the reasons for missing their sales target provides an opportunity to understand both internal and external challenges – and seek countermeasures to these.

Common external factors include:

- Economic fluctuations

- Market condition changes

- Customer preference shifts

- New or increased competition

Common internal factors could be:

- Inadequate training

- Insufficient motivation

- Inefficient sales processes

The way you approach the question can seriously impact the success of this endeavour. For example, bluntly asking: "What went wrong?" encourages scapegoating and puts everyone on the defensive. Instead, try asking: "In what ways can we create greater success in the future?" This forward-looking, positive orientation is a lot more constructive and inspiring than the "What did you do wrong?" approach.

Again, a productive starting point for these meetings is: "In similar circumstances in the past, what worked really well for us?" This engages the team or individuals in creating a strategy to overcome these challenges in the future instead of allowing them to dwell on the negative. Follow this with: "What could we do more of, based on what we learned from the review?" If you're having trouble setting a positive tone in these performance assessments, you may want to look into the concept of "appreciative inquiry" developed by Cooperrider and Suresh Srivastva in the 1980s. (A good book on the subject is *Conversations Worth Having* by Jackie Stavros and Cheri Torres.) The key point is that these round-table meetings do not need to be just about correcting your course to pursue your business vision more efficiently. Done correctly, they are a great way to motivate and inspire a team, whether they are currently doing better than expected or missing the mark somewhat.

Even if your team is hitting and exceeding targets with ease, performance review meetings still present an opportunity to examine internal and external reasons for their success. Understanding the causes involved means you can replicate these conditions and tactics in the future. The same methods and tools may well play an integral part in your company's future performance; they may even be added to your regular business processes.

Meetings Fostering Collaboration and Results

Poorly planned and led meetings are a brake on productivity, not just in terms of the hours they take up but by lowering attendees' motivation and causing them to lose focus. It doesn't have to be that way, though: when meetings are organized around a specific purpose and everyone feels empowered to have their say, they multiply the effectiveness of your team. This is another example of how keeping your business vision at the forefront supports success.

Meetings are opportunities to come together as *one* team and build *one* collective win. Although some companies have bad reputations for scheduling too many meetings, this is really a symptom of having the wrong kinds of meetings. Well-conducted, structured conversations can serve as valuable platforms for communication and collaboration. In an effective meeting, information is shared, decisions are made, problems are solved, and constructive feedback is given.

Good meetings foster teamwork, align individuals with organizational goals, and facilitate accountability. Just as importantly, meetings can boost motivation and promote team-building. The key is to structure and conduct the meetings so that they benefit the team. This means setting clear objectives and agendas, as well as striking a balance between frequency and duration to avoid wasting time unnecessarily.

Too Few Meetings Can Mean Missed Opportunities

Small businesses tend to have fewer meetings rather than too many. This can even be the case for larger organizations that started off as very small teams and grew organically. There used to be no need for formal meetings because the people you needed to speak to were just a desk or two away. As the organization grows, though, the need to keep up with a growing team means that a habit of calling regular meetings has to evolve.

The risk of not having sufficient meetings is that essential communication simply won't take place. Assuming that every individual will seek out and talk to everyone affected by or involved in their work can easily lead to disappointment. Information ends up being siloed, which inevitably causes misalignment of goals and actions rather than your team working harmoniously. A common result is that your team splits into various groups that communicate regularly among themselves but less often with other team members, leading to work being duplicated as well as missed opportunities for collaboration or innovation.

Another overlooked but just as risky problem is that teams are not receiving feedback and are exposed to only limited opportunities for learning and professional development. This can impede individual and organizational growth, especially if some of your team members lack experience. This can also result in a lack of cohesiveness and loyalty. When people don't feel like they belong to something greater than themselves, it increases the chance of people seeing the organization as a temporary stop on a career journey rather than part of their long-term future.

Regular meetings with well-established expectations will help you to achieve your desired outcomes, bring your team closer together, and avoid opportunities being missed through a lack of communication.

The Problem with Ineffective Meetings

Ineffective meetings are a significant drain on individual and organizational productivity. If you have ever worked in a corporate environment, you may well have experienced this first-hand. It can feel like you spend most of your working hours in meetings with no point and no goals. It seems that nothing is accomplished by all this talking and listening and there is no time left to do the actual work.

Ineffective meetings generally amount to nothing but a waste of time simply because they lack clear agendas and structures. Without a well-defined purpose, there is a sense of aimlessness, and pointless digressions, long but unfocused speeches, and other forms of time wastage are more likely. Attendees may struggle to stay engaged and fail to see the relevance of their contributions.

Another common factor that makes meetings ineffective is poor facilitation and leadership. More strident voices overshadow others and discussions go off-track as dominant personalities raise issues regarding their own needs rather than following the set agenda. One additional issue to watch out for is if nobody takes any follow-up actions even after a great and apparently productive meeting. If this is a common occurrence, participants enter meetings already frustrated, feeling like their time is only going to be squandered instead of resulting in tangible outcomes.

Establish Effective Meetings That Actualize Your Business Vision

Effective meetings are well-timed discussions and forums for feedback. They allow the sharing of pertinent information and give all of us an opportunity to hold each other accountable to our collective goals. They identify challenges before they can become problems and allow for collaborative solutions. By the time they leave the conference room or video call, everyone is on the same page and part of a unified team.

Clear communication during meetings fosters a shared understanding of goals, strategies, and expectations among attendees. Everyone knows what is expected of them and every other member of the team. They know how their progress will be tracked and appreciate the importance of their role in the grand scheme of things. Resources can be allocated effectively because everyone knows where you are collectively and where you're aiming to be. Everyone is rowing in the same direction.

Meetings that encourage active participation also build relationships and trust within teams and between departments. This, by itself, is a major boost in the effectiveness of communication in a company. Well-run meetings facilitate the exchange of ideas and give every voice space to be heard. They can also nurture creativity and innovation within the organization by providing a safe space for out-of-the-box thoughts.

Take a moment here to think about meetings in your organization. Do they meet the criteria of successful meetings discussed above? Which elements does your business need to tweak to make them more effective?

Essential Meetings

Whether your business currently has too many meetings or too few, the way to move forward is to establish which are essential and institute them. As you will see, these regular meetings serve a clear purpose and move your vision forward. They are not just formalities or opportunities to spout hot air.

Some common examples of essential meetings are:

- **Quarterly and Annual Meetings** – These meetings evaluate progress towards the vision, three-year strategic objectives, and annual goals. Budgets and plans can be made according to progress on an organizational and departmental level. All leaders should be present so that the organization can obtain insights from across the business and adapt where necessary. These high-level meetings also provide an opportunity to update the vision and goals if the environment is changing.

- **Process Review Meetings** – Regular reviews of your business processes, first by department and then collectively as a team, allow you to continuously firm up best practices and adjust what isn't working. Review and revision of processes can be ongoing, with periodical meetings scheduled to get everyone on the same page.

- **Training and Development Meetings** – Frequent training and development meetings narrow the gap between where the team currently is and where they need to be. Most people require some support in acquiring the capabilities they'll need to actualize the vision.

- **Townhall Meetings** – Townhall meetings allow your organization to celebrate collective achievements that bring you closer to the shared vision. Be generous in your praise and kudos and acknowledge the successes of specific teams and individuals in your company. You can also use this time to explain and clarify company-wide initiatives you've previously, or soon will, share in writing. These all-hands meetings also provide a forum for employee questions. The main purpose of gathering together as a group in this way is to boost morale, build trust, and create a sense of belonging.

- **One-to-one meetings:** These were mentioned in Chapter 10, where we examined the kind of leadership needed to scale up a small business; we'll also discuss them in more detail below. Basically, one-on-one meetings provide an essential connection and feedback loop between leaders and their direct reports. Spending some time with each individual supports the team's day-to-day work and also increases their job satisfaction.

- **Personal Growth Program:** As discussed in Chapter 11, on building an elite team, people are the strongest asset that we have. It stands to reason that we cannot grow our business unless we take care of our people's growth as well.

One-on-One Meetings

We spoke of the benefits of scheduling regular one-on-one meetings with all your direct reports in an earlier chapter. Some people aren't entirely comfortable speaking up in a group environment; individual conversations are a great way to establish connection and alignment. These meetings are also an important vehicle for personal and professional development.

Taking these meetings seriously helps to foster a trusting relationship. One-on-one meetings should be held as frequently as is efficient; once per week is a good standard. Leaders who regularly meet with their direct reports and understand their motivations and aspirations tend to have a team with strong job satisfaction and, therefore, strong growth potential and longer retention. How, then, should you structure and guide these meetings?

Preceded by Report

I recommend looking over a short report template filled in by your direct reports before each one-on-one meeting. What information do you need to support their success at work and even outside? Getting this in writing will help you highlight the most important issues. A template for you to tweak and expand on follows:

Weekly Primary Deliverable Number:

Your Successes:

Your Challenges:

Your Opportunities:

Your Personal Well-being:

Other Comments:

Focus on Their Success

Starting each meeting with a short conversation about their well-being in general, even outside work, can be an important source of connection and motivation. We all bring all of ourselves to work, and an obstacle in one area of our life affects all others. Our personal and professional lives blend into each other. A leader who cares about the team's well-being in a holistic sense earns trust and loyalty. This all starts with taking time to have regular conversations.

The benefits of creating unity are too great to allow any leader in your company to hide behind the excuse of being too busy to hold regular one-on-one meetings with each of their direct reports. Losing valuable team members due to job dissatisfaction or unresolved issues is just too much of a missed opportunity. The time leaders will spend hiring and training replacements, or dealing with complaints when they drop the ball, is far greater than having short weekly or even monthly meetings with everyone they're leading.

Structure More Effective Meetings

There are five elements that characterize every effective meeting:

- Follow a predefined agenda with a duration allocated for each item.

- Drive alignment with the vision and goals of the organization.

- Actively pursue progress toward the vision.

- Address challenges and mine opportunities.

- Encourage open and honest communication while promoting the overall success of the business.

An emphasis on your business vision and goals is key to running effective meetings. As discussed in previous chapters, keeping your eyes on the prize is central to unifying your team. Reporting, communication, strategic planning, and in fact every aspect of your work should be based on your vision. When everybody knows where the boat is heading, they row that much harder and with confidence in their organization.

A predefined meeting agenda with a clear outcome should be established for all meetings, ad hoc or regular. This, along with any relevant performance data, is shared ahead of time so that participants are fully prepared by the time they arrive. A carefully scheduled agenda can even become a kind of routine: following the same predefined schedule for recurring meetings establishes clear expectations, continuity, and efficiency.

Here is an example of an efficient agenda for weekly sales team meetings. Note how each item occupies a defined time slot, preventing a loss of focus and momentum. Let's see how this may look in practice:

Meeting name: Weekly sales team meeting

Meeting objective:

1. Keeping track of the team's portion of the vision and making sure they are aligned with the goals of the organization.

2. Mine opportunities from the past week's challenges and wins.

Frequency: Every Monday morning, 9:30-10:20 a.m., unless rescheduled to accommodate holidays and any unusual circumstances.

Meeting intention: Open, supportive, and concise communication.

Standing agenda:

- Celebration (9:30-9:35 AM): Review our clients' wins of the week!

- Goals and actions review (9:35-9:50 AM): Briefly review the team's contribution to the organization's goals in terms of the business vision and collect discussion items.

- Accountability numbers (9:50-10:00 AM): Go over the sales report from last week and track the team's work. This provides an overview of the team's performance and identifies any areas needing attention.

- Challenges and opportunities (10:00 – 10:15): Decide on which items from the above would benefit from a team discussion and address them.

- Summary of the meeting (10:15-10:20): Agree on the follow-up items from the meeting and designate their owners. The team reviews the action items from the previous week's meeting to ensure progress and completion.

End of the meeting (10:20)

That's a lot to pack into 50 minutes, yet that is what an efficient meeting looks like. Let's take a close look at the above meeting structure:

Meeting name: Weekly sales team meeting

Just by reading the meeting name, the participants and frequency are clear.

Meeting objective:

1. Keeping track of the team's portion of the vision and making sure they are aligned with the goals of the organization.

2. Mine opportunities from the past week's challenges and wins.

When we set clear meeting objectives, everyone understands what the meeting is about and, therefore, what they should be prepared for in order to make a relevant contribution. Having a clear purpose makes it easy for the person facilitating the meeting to bring people back on topic by reminding them of the meeting objectives. The standing agenda should reflect what you as a group are trying to accomplish.

Frequency: Every Monday morning, 9:30-10:20 a.m., unless rescheduled to accommodate holidays and any unusual circumstances.

Scheduling a recurring meeting ensures that people can make room for it in their calendars. Whenever possible, try to keep regular meetings at the same time because it makes scheduling easier. Participants also become more familiar with the structure and agenda, so they know how to contribute effectively.

The start and end time of the meeting is noted here so that people know what to expect and can plan their other tasks around it. Training your team to value time as their most precious resource will benefit both the organization and the individuals. People are more likely to be on time and stick to relevant topics if they know that a limited duration is involved. You don't need to automatically default to half-hour or one-hour meeting durations. If you schedule more time than is needed, people will fill the time chitchatting. This is not a negative outcome in itself, but neither does it have anything to do with organizing an effective meeting.

In the standing agenda, approximate timelines are given for each section so meeting attendees can see which topics are consistently addressed and how much time is given to each. This gives a clear signal of what is regarded as important. Your team will work ever so much harder at what matters, knowing that their role's primary deliverable numbers will be reviewed and both their wins and challenges will be discussed. Weekly meetings, along with regular reports, provide accountability. Leaders and team members alike will share their performance and progress on deliverables.

Meeting intention: Open, supportive, and concise communication.

Consider what would be the most appropriate intention for the meeting based on its type, your company values, and the team. This may vary from organization to organization and time to time. A one-on-one meeting concerning an employee's welfare may be more expansive, whereas a weekly sales review will be narrower in scope and more direct in terms of what is discussed.

Also, keep in mind that the intention alone will not promote "open, supportive, and concise communication". However, stating this upfront encourages the right attitude and provides a reminder the facilitator can point back to if things get off-track.

Here is one example of how setting a clear intention can help effective meetings. In my coaching, my clients and I set an intention for our coaching sessions during our first meeting. We call this "designing the alliance". One such intention we establish is being concise; we agree to a cue – "bottom line" – if either of us feel that the other party is moving away from the topic at hand. It is easy to get sidetracked by anecdotes and stories that don't really speak to the point, so referring back to our stated intention helps both of us to use the coaching time wisely.

Celebration (9:30-9:35 AM): Review our clients' wins of the week!

Celebration is the segment of time when clients' wins are shared and team members are given kudos for their successes. By celebrating positive outcomes for your clients, you reinforce the business's core purpose and mission by focusing on the positive impact you are creating for all stakeholders. Starting off the meeting on this note is extremely invigorating for those in your team.

Many of them will have joined your company because they believe in its purpose. Celebrating progress toward it unites the team behind common goals from the very beginning and sets the tone for the rest of your time together. It can also serve as an important learning opportunity for newer members, showing them what kinds of actions are seen as important.

Goals and actions review (9:35-9:50 AM): Briefly review the team's contribution to the organization's goals in terms of the business vision and collect discussion items. This lets everyone know what their colleagues are busy with and ensures that everybody on board is rowing in the same direction.

Accountability numbers (9:50-10:00 AM): Go over the sales report from last week and track the team's work. This provides an overview of the team's performance and identifies any areas needing attention.

In the preceding "Goals and actions review", we looked over the reports outlining individual progress toward the business's vision, goals, and actions. They will have been analyzed by each individual before the meeting, so all meeting participants will already know their contents. While these reports contain individual accounts of weekly performance, this portion of the meeting is not concerned with rehashing this information. Instead, we will focus on how the team can support each other. Issues and concerns emerging from the reports are discussed and ways are found to convert them into opportunities.

The key to remaining effective and on task here is to not analyze each challenge and opportunity in depth; simply identifying them may be enough. Where more insight is needed, this can be generated in the next part of the meeting or a separate brainstorming session. The priority is simply to check everyone's deliverable numbers and list the challenges and opportunities you experienced during the past week. You will be able to identify issues that may warrant another meeting, with its own intention and agenda, while others can be quickly resolved during the next portion of the current meeting. You will want to keep a special eye out for recurring issues or new business opportunities.

Challenges and opportunities (10:00 – 10:15): Decide on which items from the previous segment would benefit from a team discussion and address them.

Look over the discussion items that came up during the previous section of the meeting. The team should be able to agree on which ones can be resolved during the allotted fifteen minutes, which warrant a separate meeting, and which ones can be actioned later the same day. Examples of plans that can be implemented as soon as the meeting breaks up can be an email to address a customer's concern, booking a future training session, or bringing a problem to the attention of another department.

The fifteen-minute timeframe allows the team to stick to the point rather than wasting time on anecdotes and irrelevancies. You can address each item briefly and agree on the best course of action before swiftly moving on to the next. Providing a tight, hard-and-fast time limit communicates that the weekly sales meeting is not the place to commiserate about a challenge you are facing. Instead, it is where solutions and responses to challenges are established.

Summary of the meeting (10:15-10:20): Agree on the follow-up items from the meeting and designate their owners. The team reviews the action items from the previous week's meeting to ensure progress and completion.

Meetings alone don't create effectiveness. The true value of meetings only becomes apparent when you have acted on the agreed-upon follow-up items. Wrap up each meeting by discussing these and assign an owner and timeline to each one. Everyone will then be aware of who is responsible for what and progress can be reviewed in the "goals and action review" of next week's meeting.

Processes of Repeatable Success

If you are like many of us, you and your team may tend to do things the same way you always have, both in our personal and professional lives. Often, it is not because those approaches are the most effective or efficient, but simply because we are creatures of habit. We never stopped to ask if there is a more efficient way to do it.

Businesses, too, can fall victim to this kind of inertia. In the past, we established processes based on the information, tools, and resources we had available to us at the time. However, if we don't audit our processes regularly, we may fail to see that the business environment, technology, and our team have changed and there are more effective ways to do certain things.

The whole point of having business processes is that they are worth repeating precisely because they improve productivity and efficiency. By reviewing reports and discussing opportunities regularly in meetings, you will be able to spot areas where common procedures can be improved and audit your business processes.

Establish Essential Business Processes

What business processes do you currently have established? If your answer is "none", this is a great time to create them. Optimizing your routines and methods is essential even if you are currently a one-person operation. You will become more efficient and productive when you start using pre-determined, thoughtfully designed processes, and create a few templates to help you handle frequently occurring situations.

For example, instead of writing a brand-new response to every single new client inquiry, you can create a form letter that contains all the information a client needs to know and can be customized if needed. By spending sufficient time, once, to ensure the quality and effectiveness of this form letter (or several), you save several minutes whenever a potential client emails you. Instead of spending half an hour composing a new response, customizing the template for each customer will take only a minute or two.

As your business grows, the time and resources saved by well-designed processes multiply, improving efficiency and productivity exponentially. These processes also standardize how things are done in your business, thus providing consistency for your clients and maintaining quality. If we think about the client inquiry above, imagine if every salesperson was crafting different responses to each email they received. The quality of communication, response time, and time spent writing the email would be dictated by the salesperson. Consistency is hard to achieve in such an environment, necessitating additional work to correct mistakes. This is a classic example of busyness triumphing over true productivity.

Defining and documenting procedures, workflows, and guidelines allow organizations to streamline operations, minimizing errors, improve control, and enhance productivity. Entrepreneurs have an easier time scaling their businesses when their processes allow for easy replication. Employees have a standard procedure they can follow and documented processes they can turn to if they need guidance. This way, they can spend more mental energy dealing with unusual situations, as most day-to-day issues will be routine. Your team will be more orientated to the future and customers' needs, which are always goals to strive for.

What constitutes your essential business processes? Common ones include marketing, sales, registration or booking, customer service, and operations. Take a good look at how you approach common tasks now and think of ways to make your actions more efficient.

Document Business Processes

When formalizing each process, the goal is to standardize workflows, improve the consistency of our products and services, and make our operations more efficient and productive. Some processes, like administrative procedures governed by government regulations or industry standards, may need to be very detailed and prescriptive. Other processes can allow more leeway.

Document each business process by writing down the essential steps and providing links to templates and supporting material. These documents are shared within your organization and communicate new and existing procedures. There are two different approaches you can take:

1. A step-by-step Microsoft Help-style document that employees can follow along without anyone assisting or training them. This type of documentation has to be comprehensive and detailed.

2. A simpler, macro-level process that outlines essential steps and provides supporting templates but doesn't prescribe every detail and leaves room for employee discretion.

Tackle one process at a time. Start by describing each in a one-page document and expand from there, if necessary. Think of auditing your business processes as an exercise in expediting your productivity. It's worthwhile creating and scheduling S.M.A.R.T. goals to establish or update your business processes.

Once a process has been created, designate an owner to maintain it. This individual will be responsible for reviewing their process and checking if it is efficient, effective, and up to date. The owner will do this periodically, seeking input from others where necessary. They are also responsible for updating the process documentation and ensuring that changes are communicated.

In summary, your processes of success ensure that you are taking steps toward your ambitious vision every day by creating milestones, tracking them through reports, and creating continuous opportunities through meetings. Your resounding success does not lie only in your vision, nor in your strategic plans alone, but in the plans and actions you and your team work on together. The processes are your guide in this.

Your Action:

Install Your Processes of Success – Discover what works for your business, refine, document, and replicate it.

In preparation for scaling up your business, you should move away from ad-hoc solutions to common problems. Instead, using your vision and strategic goals as a starting point, you can schedule effective meetings that promote solution-oriented thinking and employee development. Appropriate reports can provide accountability, while efficient, documented processes enable growth.

1. Review your three-year strategic goals and your yearly goals.

2. Plan actions toward your goals. A recurring meeting will help to accomplish this task.

3. Schedule essential meetings in your team's calendar.

4. Record your goals and actions in your team's agreed-upon platform with an owner for each action.

5. Establish reports and meetings to achieve the above goals and track actions.

6. Establish business processes that ensure operational efficiency and productivity and schedule periodical reviews and training.

CONCLUSION

In *The 7 Habits of Highly Effective People*, Stephen Covey says: "If the ladder is not leaning against the right wall, every step we take just gets us to the wrong place faster." It is my hope that this book has helped you to place your ladder against the right wall before continuing your journey. When you do so, when you create a business that is in alignment with your definition of overall life success, your life is the master that your business serves. Succeeding in business is a great achievement, but it is still only a means to other, more important ends.

When the opposite is true, and your business goals are divorced from and not harmonized with your definition of overall life success, then there is a great danger of leaning the ladder up against one of many wrong walls – size, money, success and so on. A bigger company, lots more money, and a successful company with a great reputation aren't bad in themselves, of course. Before you start ascending those rungs, however, you need to consider a dilemma most people never think about. Business achievements don't bring you happiness when they aren't connected to your life fulfillment.

Your business easily becomes the master that your life serves. This represents a complete reverse of what most people, in their heart of hearts, desire. The only possible result is a life filled with compromises. While you are building a company that's in conflict with your personal vision, you will experience a lack of fulfillment and work/life balance. By the time you finish your business journey, there's every chance that you will feel disappointed rather than elated. Considering that entrepreneurs start their businesses as a means to create a fulfilling life, it is remarkable how often our priorities can get switched.

The more holistic approach I advocate for places your life success first. Establishing and scaling up your business is a supporting goal, the leaning of your ladder against the right wall. Succeeding will establish a thriving life that you have the privilege to claim as your own. You will be more fulfilled than ever. That's a bold promise, but it's one that I am confident is within your reach.

I know it works. It has worked for my clients and it worked for me. This process has allowed me to construct a life and a business in which I am living my core values. I have built a business where I earn money by helping people to define and actualize lives that they love to live. Having achieved my financial freedom a decade prior, my business success is motivated by my desire to help more people. I do this both through coaching clients through the process of bringing their dreams to life and by using the resulting profits to practice more philanthropy.

My business goals never eclipse my life outside of working hours, though. I see my business and the fulfillment it brings as just one aspect of my full and rich life. I am present with my loved ones and have surrounded myself with people who inspire and motivate me. Equally, I hope that I inspire and motivate them, as well as many others through mentoring and volunteering. I live in a beautiful country that aligns with my values and where it is easy to indulge in my hobbies, particularly outdoor pursuits such as hiking and gardening. I am living my dream life now; I firmly believe that you, too, can live yours.

My hope for you is that reading this book gives you the confidence to dream audaciously, both personally and professionally. When your ambitions excite you, planning and executing them is no longer a chore. It's like planning a dream holiday: the process of planning is almost as exciting as the trip itself. You look forward to laying out your itinerary and feel energized following each planning session. If your personal and business visions are inspiring and exciting, then even time spent plotting a course to your destination is exciting.

I hope that you will apply the SCALE-UP system described in this book in order to start feeling in greater control of both your life and your business. Feelings of being overwhelmed can send even the most organized person to a place of anxiety, stress, and sleepless nights. It's impossible to be effective in that state of being. Defining your personal and business visions and building your unique productivity system will put you back in control. It's not easy to stick to our schedule because it takes time to unlearn habits and establish new ones. I promise you, however, that the rewards of making regular progress are huge, so start now and stick to your new routine.

I wrote this book while undergoing treatment for breast cancer. This was perhaps the biggest emotional challenge of my life. I was already convinced that we can and must define, build, and live our fulfilling lives. Having been forced to confront the fragility of human life, I'm even more convinced that we need to act on our dreams now: not tomorrow, not later, but today.

It hurts me when I see people who don't even entertain the possibility of making their dream life a reality. As a result, most don't even try. By reading this book, you have already shown more ambition than the vast majority of people. Use that ambition to spring into action, now. Yes, the same opportunities will probably still exist in 24 hours. But there's no reason not to grasp them now.

You started your SCALE-UP journey by first establishing your life success by defining the four pillars of what it means to you to be a thriving person. Once this is done, you're well on your way to practising self-leadership. You will know your destination and have a pretty clear idea of how to get there. These are the four pillars you need to pay attention to:

- **Life purpose** – The positive impact you want to have on the world. What is the "why?" behind what you do and the things you care about? We identified the people who are important to us and the kind of legacy we would like to leave behind in this world.

- **Core values** – The compass that points you in the right direction. What are the values and guiding principles that will illuminate the path leading to your destination? This section identified your core values and then turned them into guiding principles to determine how they will come alive on a day-to-day basis.

- **Life vision** – The destination you are working toward. What does a thriving life, in which different elements support each other in a harmonious way, look like for you? We looked at the various elements of your life and took stock of how fulfilling each element is, so we could identify what would make each element even more fulfilling. Your big, ambitious, exciting life vision was distilled down to one leverage goal and one supporting goal so that you can focus on making progress.

- **Productivity system** – The actions that will bring you closer to your destination. How can you ensure that you are prioritizing your vision on a daily, weekly, and monthly basis rather than letting everyday distractions blow you off course? We looked at putting time aside in your calendar to plan and make regular progress toward your goals. These goals were also broken down into smaller compounding actions that you can build habits around.

Understanding and applying these four pillars benefits you in two principal ways. The first is that you know what your thriving life looks like and what you need to do to achieve it. This allows you to use your business to support your life rather than sacrificing your life to support your business. Remember: financial success is only one part of your ideal life. If you have to deny yourself fulfillment in order to make money, your ladder is leaning against the wrong wall.

The second advantage of embracing self-leadership is that someone who knows who they are and what is important to them is automatically a more effective business leader. As you add more people to your elite team, you need to become less of a rower and more of a helmsman. As I often say: "Without a productive leader, there is no productive business." When you are productive as a person, you are better equipped to build a productive, elite team, who then together build a productive business. Stakeholders will recognize your ambition and values, leading to all sorts of synchronous events that move you closer to the actualization of your vision.

The second part of the SCALE-UP framework established what constitutes a productive business and what you need in place to achieve your definition of it. With your map and compass in hand, the next step is to construct an efficient boat to get you to your destination. This shouldn't be done willy-nilly, though: an inspiring business culture – which is an essential prerequisite for sustainable growth – rests on four important supports. These are:

- **Core strengths** – The pillars that support your culture and help you give an identity to your tribe. Your business core purpose defines the impact your business seeks to make on the world. Your business core values guide how your company and the people in the organization conduct themselves. Your business core focus identifies your specialty based on what you can do best and what will be profitable both now and in the future. Your core purpose, values, and focus all mutually support one another.

- **Ambitious vision** – With your core business strengths established, you can use these to create an ambitious vision for your company's future. Your ambitious vision should be a "big, hairy, audacious goal" that gets you and your team excited about what the future holds. During this important exercise, we also created your three-year strategic objectives and Year 1, 2, and 3 goals toward your ambitious vision. These are major steps toward and enablers of your vision. Achieving each of them constitutes a major milestone towards your ideal life.

- **Leadership** – The ways in which you can lead your team to achieve your shared vision. Let's be clear: there are very few "born leaders". Leadership is a skill that's developed and practised. There are going to be a few false starts and embarrassing moments. The more important part of leadership is embracing what works and discarding the rest. This starts with ensuring that you are creating win-win situations in all interactions with stakeholders. You can build better relationships with your team and clients by "communicating to connect" rather than "communicating to respond". We also explored how to hold teams accountable in a way that supports their work and life success and how to develop effective leaders within your business.

- **Elite team** – The ideal team that you need to actualize your shared vision. When you visualize having achieved your ambitious vision, what are the roles that are essential to business operations? What are the skills needed in each position to consistently meet and exceed your goals? What values and ambitions does each team member need to internalize to become one of your tribe? We identified the roles that your business needs to have in place in the next three years in order to achieve your three-year strategic goals. We then identified the primary deliverable for that role and the skills and qualities necessary to be successful in it. From there, gap analysis will allow you to look objectively at what changes need to be made in the next three years. This could include training your existing staff, moving staff to roles where they may thrive, or hiring new employees that galvanize your existing team.

The final part of the SCALE-UP framework revolves around the tools vital to actualizing the exciting plans you have for your business. These include getting your team united behind your shared vision by identifying win-win scenarios and creating processes of success.

- **Unity** – Focus begets unity and vice versa. A unified team makes achieving your ambitious vision a smooth process; a disunified team means that you'll spend way too much of your precious time and energy putting out fires and correcting avoidable mistakes. A sure sign of a unified team is that everyone is rowing in unison and in the same direction. We broke this complex concept into three parts: unity behind your vision, processes, and accountability. This starts with getting your team's buy-in in the visioning process. Engagement is the key to getting buy-in.

- **The processes of success** – The processes of success ensure that your vision doesn't stay in a drawer; rather, it gets actualized. It is discernible in your daily business operations. Milestones, goals and actions are created, scheduled, and shared with the team. Performance and ownership are tracked using a platform and calendar the team commits to. Reports and meetings are predefined and established to promote accountability, communication, and opportunity mining. In addition, documented processes ensure optimized operations that can easily be scaled: what has proven to be successful is tweaked to ensure your continued success. Business processes are established and continuously evolved to garner success in an ever-changing environment.

I have carefully avoided saying that any of this is easy. Scaling up a business is not easy. Very little of consequence is. What I have tried to do instead is break down the process of scaling up a small business into manageable steps. Interrogating yourself as to your core values isn't easy; becoming a leader that guides, develops, and chooses members of an elite team isn't easy. Yet, the process of doing so, and certainly the results, are always worth it. I often say that we shouldn't live our lives by default, but by design. Taking deliberate action is what brings us happiness. What aspect of the SCALE-UP system are you most excited about right now?

If you have taken the action steps attached to each chapter, you will already be well on your way. If you haven't, a good place to start is by creating your personal productivity routine. It doesn't matter if you're a one-person operation or already managing a large team. Setting aside time each week and going over the action items, planning and actioning, on a daily or weekly basis can be your next step. Again: we are not aiming at easy wins. When constructing your ideal life, a lot of what you need to do is hard. The key is to work towards what matters. You can be busy all day long without achieving anything; let's try to avoid that by placing your vision at the centre of all you do. You won't achieve all your goals at once. Instead, let's work towards your objectives one day at a time using a proven system for success.

Don't wait until tomorrow. Start the process today. Design your ideal life in which both personal and professional dreams work together in harmony, and then make that thriving life a reality. Even your most audacious dreams are within your grasp if you break them down into achievable goals and prioritize these in your schedule. There are going to be obstacles and setbacks; this is simply part of life. As I mentioned at the beginning of this book, I cannot tell you what kind of success you will achieve. I am certain, however, that it is within your grasp.

Just remember: Don't be busy. Be productive!

My website contains some resources about scaling businesses, leadership, and related topics. For additional support, you can also email me at scale@sustainablelifedesign.com. I do appreciate honest feedback, whether directly or in the form of book reviews.

ACKNOWLEDGEMENT

I'm deeply grateful to many people with whom I've shared my life path, for a short or long while, in a professional context or otherwise. I learnt a great deal about what it means to be a good listener and communicator, effective leader and thriving entity. My former colleagues, coaching clients, friends, mentors, and mentees all played a huge role in my education and learning.

I want to say special thanks to my life partner Håkan Björn for his steadfast and enthusiastic support in anything that I do. You are the true definition and embodiment of what it means to be an inspiring partner. I am endlessly grateful for the love and partnership we share.

I also want to share my deep sense of gratitude for my clients for trusting me during their journey to their next level of achievement, allowing me to develop my SCALE-UP framework while giving me feedback and encouragement. Through your earnest aspirations and development, I and my coaching skills grew. I'd also like to thank them for showing such generosity in their hearts during my cancer treatment program. Thank you for cheering me on and for being flexible with my schedule during chemo, surgery, radiation, and all the doctors' appointments. You managed to make the journey so far incredibly rewarding and you are a source of inspiration and fulfillment.

Thank you, Rachel, for your generosity in allowing me to share your stories freely with the readership. You are an exceptional example of a thriving small business owner and I'm confident your story will resonate with and inspire many other entrepreneurs.

I'm also thankful for the talented individuals who supported me in writing this book. You have proven to be instrumental in bringing my thoughts into print. Thank you!

I couldn't have written this book without any of you.

Linda Chung

www.ingramcontent.com/pod-product-compliance
Lightning Source LLC
Chambersburg PA
CBHW071201210326
41597CB00016B/1630